CW00349099

Sunco Safari

Non-Fiction

Copyright

© John Abrahams. 2006

All rights reserved

No parts of this publication may be reproduced, stored in a retrieval system, or transmitted in any form or by any means, electronic, mechanical, photocopying, recording or otherwise without the prior permission of the copyright owner.

British Library Cataloguing In Publication Data
A Record of this Publication is available
 from the British Library

ISBN 1846853893
978-1-84685-389-0

First Published 2006 by

Exposure Publishing, an imprint of Diggory Press,
Three Rivers, Minions, Liskeard, Cornwall, PL14 5LE, UK
WWW.DIGGORYPRESS.COM

Sunco Safari

By

John Abrahams

In Memory of Ian

Introduction

*A**frica:** From the mountains of the Ethiopian Highlands, which feed the Blue Nile, to the gigantic Sahara Desert with it's awesome desolate beauty. From the Equatorial jungles of the west to the seemingly endless grassy savannah plains of the east, which stretch down the side of the continent, trying to hold back the ever-encroaching arid deserts of the Kalahari and Namid in the southwest. Africa is indeed a vast continent of mystery and adventure.*

Attached precariously to the birthplace of civilization by a small piece of land at Suez, the northern lands were populated and explored over thousands of years; but the great barrier of the Sahara and the extreme difficulties of negotiating the Cataracts of the upper Nile, meant that exploration of the rest of this continent did not happen until the 19th century. The Royal Geographical Society of Britain sponsored explorers like Livingstone and Stanley. In their quest to find the source of the Nile River, they started to map parts of the east and south of this great continent. As a boy I used to read in the National Geographic Magazine about these foreign lands and often dreamed of travelling to such places.

It is difficult to gauge how big Africa is. It is the only continent on earth to be crossed by the equator and both the tropics of Cancer and Capricorn. A great natural fault in the earth's surface leaves a huge scar, which runs down nearly the whole continent. It was to the area just east of the famous African Rift Valley, near to the Equator, that our journey was to take us. This is a land of big game, different peoples and various cultures.

The mid 1960s saw the early independence of Kenya from British rule, following the Mau Mau rebellion. A relative peace was also helped by the country being a member of the Commonwealth, and still being influenced by the generations of colonial rule. It was under this situation that three friends and I were to make a journey that was to be a trip of a lifetime. We were fortunate to be able to travel and explore this fascinating land in relative freedom and safety.

It is good to travel, and see this wonderful earth; perhaps to those more remote parts away from the busy commercial tourist holiday centres.

"But it is good to remember:
Leave only a footprint
Take only a photograph
But keep a memory."

John Abrahams

.

| Frank | Ian | John | Andrew |
| Rothera | Priddin | Abrahams | Todd |

Contents

<u>Part One</u>

The Journey

Route Schedule

Stafford to Athens
Outward

[1966]			
Thurs.	12.50 hrs	Stafford	Depart
4th Aug.	18.30 hrs	Dover	
	20.00 hrs		Sailed on Chantillly
	21.15 hrs	Calais	Depart
Frid.	05.30 hrs	Saarbrucken	German Border
5th Aug.	07.45 hrs	Black Forest	Breakfast
	12.50 hrs	Munich	850 miles in 24 hrs (10 miles from Munich)
	19.00 hrs	Radstadt	Night Halt before Radstadt
Sat.	09.25 hrs	Radstadt	Depart
6th Aug.	13.00 hrs	Loibl Summit	Highest and Steepest Mountain Pass of Journey
	18.30 hrs	Zargreb	Fuel and Meal Halt
	20.00 hrs	Zargreb	Depart
Sun.	00.00 hrs	Belgrade	Fuel Halt
7th Aug.	01.00 hrs	Belgrade	Depart
	02.00 hrs		Rejoin Motorway
	08.00 hrs	Greek Border	
	10.30 hrs	Greek Border	Depart
	16.45 hrs	Athens	2300 miles in 76 hrs

Route Schedule

Stafford to Athens
Return

Sat. 10th Sept.	09.30 hrs	Athens	Depart
		N. Greece	Carburettor flooding
	07.00 hrs	Skopje	Evening Meal
Sun. 11th Sept.		N. Greece	Carburettor flooding again. Effected cure
	06.30 hrs	Zargreb	Breakfast
	12.30 hrs	Loibl Summit	
	14.00 hrs	Klagenfurt	Repair Drive shaft coupling and suspension
	19.00 hrs	Salzsburg	Evening Meal
	21.00 hrs	German Border	
Mon. 12th Sept.	07.00 hrs	Belgium Border	
	09.30.hrs	Oostende	2000 miles in 48 hrs
	10.00 hrs	Oostende	Sailed for home
	14.00 hrs	Dover	
	21.30 hrs	Stafford	60 Hours from Athens including ferry

12

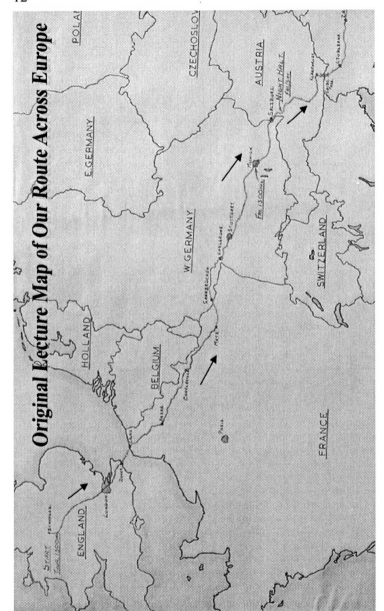

Original Lecture Map of Our Route Across Europe

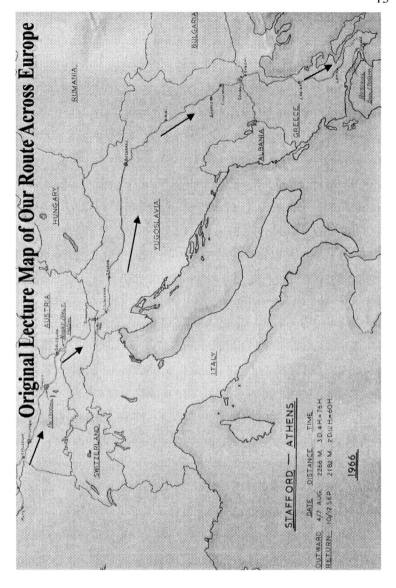

Original Lecture Map of Our Route Across Europe

Chapter 1

An Invitation

I t all started in the early spring of 1966, on a rare occasion when three of the four of us young men had been away for the weekend visiting our respective parents. We gathered as usual on Sunday evening to discuss past escapades, and to plan the next motor sport event, for motor sport had become a progressively active part of our lives for some two years or so. We were in our early twenties and all in the latter parts of our engineering apprenticeships at the English Electric Company at Stafford. We had previously lived at the apprentices' hostel at Dunston Hall near Stafford, before sharing a square mobile home-type cottage called of all things - a 'Sun Cottage'. From this we derived the name *'Sunco'*.

There were actually two of these located in the grounds behind a nice bungalow at Bednall Head on the edge of the Cannock Chase between Stafford and Cannock. Each home, set in it's own little garden, comprised of two trailers joined together making a square. One trailer was the kitchen and living room whilst the other was the bathroom and two small bedrooms. I actually slept in the second unit but effectively lived at Sun Cottage. The whole cottage was quite compact but became our home for a few years. The accommodation also had the tremendous feature of a disused hen house, which we had converted into a spacious workshop and laboratory, and of which many small firms would have been proud. This served us well, for we always seemed to have one project or other under way.

So this was how we all came to be sitting in the small lounge at Sun Cottage, planning future events, and drinking the mandatory cup of coffee and smoking the usual Embassy Regal cigarette (apart from Bunny who didn't smoke).

"When shall we go then? My folks say August is the best, between the big and the small rains". This was typical of a statement made by Frank Rothera who just assumed that we would be going. Go where? We all wondered.

"To see my folks", continued Frank with the aire of authority of a colonial upbringing.

Now Ian Priddin and Andrew 'Bunny' Todd had just returned from Yorkshire and I, John Abrahams, from Shropshire. However, Frank's folks lived in Nairobi! I should have known that something was in the air as Bert Kaempfert's 'Swinging Safari' LP record was playing on the Hi-fi.

The year before, Frank's parents, David and Edna Rothera had come back to England for a couple of months on their three-year leave break, also bringing with them Frank's younger sister Alison who at 19 years of age certainly brightened our day. We had met them several times and at a final meal out together just prior to their departure back to Kenya, they said, "You must come and see us". People often say things like that, but this was meant. Frank was holding a letter from his parents again issuing an invitation to go out to Africa!

David Rothera was a friendly sort of man who had left his family home in Nottingham to travel and work in the Far East, and then moved on to East Africa. He had worked in airport management, so consequently was able to get a reasonably priced flight for Frank. But what about us, how on earth could we get there? The three of us were dumbfounded. We just hadn't taken their original invitation seriously. We all joked and talked about it, but we all really wanted to go. How could we do it?

It is surprising how compromises happen! My dad had been telling a well-travelled friend of the family about 'John's latest project'. Now Jack Davies often journeyed a couple of hundred miles further on than most holiday makers! His attitude was for us to drive as far as we could and then fly. I put forward that suggestion and found that Ian had also been reading a book about two friends who drove to Singapore. So we all pondered about it. "If we can't afford to fly we will just have to drive there", said some bright spark.

"Take too long, we've only got two weeks hols anyway", said another. So the idea was born to do a 'fly drive'. That night we got very little sleep. My thoughts returned to articles in the National Geographic Magazines about Africa and big game and adventure. Was it still just a dream?

For the next week or so, the only topic of conversation was Kenya. Even the motor sport projects and events were put on hold as we all tried to find a way to go. Frank was insistent that we needed at least a month out there or it would not be worth going! So an appointment was made with the education officer at English Electric, Mr Harold Abrahams (no relation) who was in charge of all the apprentices. He quite quickly came back to us with an agreement: two weeks paid leave and four weeks unpaid leave, provided that we would give a lecture about our adventure to the College of Technology at Beaconside on our return. Yes we had six weeks. It was worth going!

We seriously pondered the idea of fly/drive, or in our case drive/fly. But to and from where? That was the question. The permutations of time, money and location and cost of flights to Kenya were all looked at in much detail. With Athens in the south of Greece being the favourite take off point. The route that we should take to get there was the next decision to be made. There were two choices: first, to cross France, then the Alps into Italy and eventually work our way down the east coast to Brindisi, catch a boat to one of the many ports on the west side of Greece, south of Albania, and continue the drive to Athens. The second choice was to cross France, Germany, Austria and over the Alps into the communist country of Yugoslavia and drive through that country to the northern part of Greece and then on down to Athens. A bit longer and travelling into the unknown situation of Yugoslavia, but cost wise, apart from petrol, only the English Channel ferry tickets to buy. After much deliberation, we unanimously agreed on the second choice and so the team swung into action spurred on by our goal, a lifetime's trip to Africa!

Whilst Frank gave over-sight to this new project, between reading his latest book and offering advice, the three of us found our individual expertise coming to the fore in order to complete this mammoth project in a relatively short time. Ian was unusual, for a young man of that era, in that he could type; so his administrative skills were put into action. Visas for Kenya, and as we soon discovered, for Yugoslavia were to be obtained. (Evidently it was possible to buy a visa at the border but that could cost more and take several days). I also had to get a passport! Plane tickets for the flight from Athens to Nairobi had to be purchased at about £190 each. Just the letters to the embassies kept Ian busy, plus of course, not forgetting the six different types of currency needed. We were asked not to take Kenyan currency, for the Rothera's would lend us the money and we could pay it back into their English Bank. They were considering moving to South Africa and there was a difficulty of getting money out of the country.

Bunny Todd was one of those rare people who combined his genius of electronics with the skills of a craftsman on practical matters. He was the boffin of the quartet and reminded me of the aeronautical engineer in Alistair Maclean's book *Sliderule.* As it was his Rally Hillman Imp car that we would use for the journey, Bunny rebuilt it with his usual meticulous attention to detail. They weren't exactly the most reliable car about and the return trip would be nearing five thousand miles!

From rereading the book of an overland trip to Singapore, particularly the European section, Ian was getting worried about the lack of petrol in Yugoslavia, and this was confirmed when back with the visas came a map of Yugoslavia showing the petrol stations! We didn't know if these were open for twenty-four hours a day or what, and we were concerned that there were no stations shown for 275 miles going south from Belgrade. Surely there must be petrol available south of Belgrade? and we would be covering that part of the journey at night. What was Bunny's solution to the problem? Fit another petrol tank! This was duly done with two fuel pumps as well, so we could switch from one tank to the other from inside the car whilst on the move! A roof rack was also constructed with a facility for taking two spare wheels instead of the usual one. The car was at last complete and tried out successfully over the Chase.

The job of logistics and route planning fell to me, which turned into quite a mammoth affair. Plotting a route of nearly two and a half thousand miles through six countries and traversing the Alps would entail a lot of work. Because of our involvement with rallying, the three of us were used to night driving and also reading maps etc. but nevertheless a detailed itinerary was necessary. I allowed four days before our flight from Athens, which was at midnight on the 8th August. This meant that after leaving work on Thursday afternoon and travelling over the first part of our journey, we should be in Austria by Friday evening; a night halt, and then drive straight through to Athens, which we should reach some thirty hours later. This would allow for a day to get the car put into the official customs park so that Bunny Todd could leave the country without it!

We decided to each drive in two hour stints, but to be flexible if the conditions warranted. Now, in rallying, the navigator is in charge of the car in everything but steering it! When to stop and where to go and how! So we unanimously agreed that if the navigator at the time, thought that the driver was too tired, then a fresh driver would take over without any argument. This in practice worked remarkably well and there were no problems on that account. The driver moved to navigating so the third refreshed person could then take the wheel. Using a European road atlas book marked with the route, a detailed route card was also made, giving all the necessary information such as customs posts, currency, and estimated petrol and food stops, as well as road and junction numbers for as much of the route as was possible. The French had a useful system on their road junctions, of a number to confirm the road wanted, and this number was shown on the Michelin maps along with some of the European through route numbers. This was particularly useful at night. We also made up a device, using an old camera and a till roll on which was typed the whole route! This meant that the driver could also keep a check on towns ahead on our route, even if the navigator was asleep! The driver could easily wind on the device and would also notice any difficulties coming up and if necessary, wake the navigator. Sounds Complicated? Well it worked, and we never actually got lost even on diversions. Now only three things had to be done:

1) A supply of spare parts for the car. This was arranged through a friendly Roots garage on a sale or return basis. Bunny had already acquired quite a lot of spares and necessary tools! However, it was not worth taking things that would take more than twelve hours to repair. We took of course the obligatory first aid kit and warning triangle, needed for France and Germany, but these were very common sense items anyway.

2) Films for cameras. These were purchased and we all kept to the same type, Agfa slide film, as slides were at that time the popular format. Ian, who was a very good photographer, was very pleased to be able to borrow his dad's Leica M3. Bunny had a Japanese Cannon and I had an old Zeiss Contax; so we were all well equipped.

3) Inoculations necessary for a trip into the tropics. The Yellow fever jabs had already been given to us at Birmingham. (They certainly did knock us out!) Frank had arranged through his GP at

Stafford for us all to get treated together! This made sense really as we other three were still registered at our various hometowns.

It turned out that the doctor had spent time in Kenya during his military service in the RAF, so knew all about East Africa. We took his advice and all lined up together for the various jabs including small pox, cholera, typhoid, hepatitis and variants etc. and of course not forgetting malaria, for which we took tablets. Now it is usual to pay for extra vaccinations etc. but the doctor only insisted that we bring him back a jar of *genuine Kenyan honey.* "No problem" said Frank, but even he was perplexed! We had been so focused on the journey to Athens that our ultimate destination in Africa had almost slipped our minds. We now really appreciated that we were certainly not going on a normal holiday, but to a land where everything would be so completely different.

As August approached, Bunny and Ian went home to Yorkshire for the weekend, and I to Shropshire, in order to say our goodbyes to our respective families. We were all surprised and pleased when my parents came over to Bednall, on the night before our departure, to wish us all "Bon Voyage".

Chapter 2

Twende (Let's Go)

It was a Thursday lunchtime when the three of us went to the Stychfields staff canteen at the English Electric Company for a last meal in Britain for some time, and we were joined by Frank and a few well wishers too. Word had got around that three mad lads were driving to Kenya, which was only half right anyway. We were looking a bit conspicuous dressed in our white/cream flannels and shirts. We resembled part of a cricket team rather than an expedition to foreign lands. Frank was to catch a plane from London Heathrow on the Friday and told us that he would meet us at Nairobi airport on Tuesday. After some final farewells we departed Stafford just before 1pm on the 4th August 1966 for a journey into the unknown.

Joining the M6 motorway at junction 13 we headed south to London, Dover and the Ferry to France. There was a relative quiet in the car as the motor purred south; not an awkward silence but a comfortable one, as we were all thinking about the journey and what we had let ourselves in for. I thought about how the friendship had developed between the four of us, as we were such different characters. Bunny (who didn't really like being called that and preferred Andrew – but, as that was what everyone new him as, in those days I will stick to Bunny) was the boffin of the quartet, very clever and quiet. He was of medium height, quite slim and was not of the athletic or sporting fraternity, but behind the wheel of a rally car he was a different man! Although he never took chances.

Ian was slightly taller and of medium build and was I suppose the academic one of the party, and like Bunny was not particularly fond of any sport apart from motor sport. Ian usually navigated on rallies, but did drive from time to time; a good all rounder and had an easy going but persevering type of character; a real asset on this type of trip.

Frank about 5ft 10in and slim, was very much the more outgoing personality of us all; probably because of his upbringing in different parts of the world. His ability to never want to give up and his expertise as a 'bush' mechanic proved very useful on many occasions. He was by far the quickest driver of the team, but did tend to take chances occasionally; nevertheless, Frank did have great respect for the navigator if he was accurate! However, we wouldn't see Frank for a few days! There was just the three of us at the moment.

I, like the others, had been to boarding school for my secondary education and had also been a keen swimmer, and photographer, but was never the academic type, preferring practical type of work. Nevertheless, I had to do all the normal subjects at school and these led me to an engineering apprenticeship at English Electric. Having been brought up in a motor sport environment, I was the instigator of the quartet's interest in cars as sport. We were all different characters but were gelled by our love of cars and adventure. It was certainly going to be an interesting journey.

'BANG', the car suddenly lurched and skewed a bit sideways. We were all jolted back from our different thoughts to the problem at hand. The noise of a flailing tyre which had just exploded is not a happy sound, for the car is very difficult to control, but we were fortunate that even though we were cruising at about seventy, the traffic was not too busy, so the driver managed to coax the Hillman Imp over to the hard shoulder safely. The wheel was duly changed and we got under way again. We all hoped that this was not a foretaste of things to come, as we hadn't done a hundred miles yet and we were now down to one spare tyre! On joining the north circular road round London (No M25 then) we decided to buy a new Pirelli tyre to make up our two spares. The fitters at the tyre centre were amused at Bunny's insistence of matching tyres on axles! But this was quickly done when they realised that we had a plane to catch on Monday night from Athens!

Continuing on the north circular road, passing near to the Ford motor works at Dagenham, then crossing under the Thames by the Dartford tunnel, we picked up the old staging route, the A2 that goes directly to Canterbury and finally Dover; one of the *cinque* ports facing France. Picking our way through the narrow streets of Dover, which had never been intended to carry the increasing volume of lorries and camions for the ferry across the English Channel (or if one was on the other side of the water *La Manche*) the Eastern docks were reached. We quickly obtained an open return ticket, that's optimism for you, and were told that a boat was leaving at 8pm that evening; we were thus able to get a meal at the port restaurant before departure. The last English meal we would have for many weeks.

On arriving at the customs point the polite but authoritative customs officer asked us where we were going? Picture the scene. A well used, 'English Electric grey' rally Hillman Imp car, loaded to the gunnels with three young men all wearing glasses and dressed in tropical clothing; must have looked a bit odd. But he smiled and said:

"When Mr Abrahams has signed his passport – you may leave the country".

It was not long until we had boarded the Sea Link ferry the *'Chantilly'* and embarked for France. As the boat slid out into the slight swell of the Channel, we all stood silently looking at the white cliffs of Dover, made famous by Vera Lynn's wartime song. I did wonder if I should ever see those cliffs again, a thought that was in common with thousands of men who had travelled to France and on to war. I felt grateful that I did not have to go through that mayhem. As the evening sun and light faded, those cliffs also faded away, so we searched out a comfortable quiet lounge and relaxed with a soft drink pondering the long journey ahead. Just under a couple of hours from boarding the ferry at Dover, we arrived at the port of Calais and my first look at France, in the dark.

The French customs were as equally interested in us, as were the British. We were not your normal tourist, mixed along with the odd caravan but mainly wagons. I suppose that it must have looked as if we were on some sort of expedition. Anyway we had our passports stamped with the Calais mark (not done these days) and proceeded out on to the dark streets of the town looking for the main N43 *la route national* to Metz and the German border. The car clock read 9.15pm.

In planning the route, I thought it would be best to start the European section with Ian driving, after all he was the only one of us to have actually travelled, though as a passenger, in a car on the wrong side of the road! Bunny had been to France with his parents, but no car, and I had been to the Isle of Man, to watch the TT races! So as the lively all aluminium engine purred away down the tree lined road heading south east, we passed Arras and Cambrai, where my uncle had survived the very first tank battle during the First World War, and on to Charleville. The rumble of the tyres on the French *parvée* was quite disconcerting at first, but it was mainly found in the towns. This *parvée* is the square cobblestones laid down as road and polished by centuries of traffic and it could be very slippery, particularly when wet!

The traffic was now quite light, just a few slow moving *camions* with trailers to have to blast past. I thought that they resembled giant insects crawling along the road with their feeler antennas sticking out each side at the front of the lorry. As vision is restricted for the driver of a right hand drive vehicle on the continent, overtaking needs caution, but we soon developed a system and only overtook when the navigator said to. When he said go, you went! We each had a share of the driving in France and were very aware of the rule of *'priorité à droite'* (give way to the right) from the previously heard many horror stories of tractors pulling straight out on to the main road even at night, and of the Frenchman full of vino in his 2CV Citroën. But we survived with out any mishaps.

The French drivers though did not like our white headlamps! Now the French thought that yellow headlights were the best, whilst the rest of the world thought white! You don't get quite the glare from yellow lamps, and they are quite good in fog, nevertheless nothing can compare to the lighting set up on a good rally car. Six lights all fitted with powerful halogen bulbs, (in those days the majority of cars just had standard bulbs), with 7in. Lucas 700 spot and fog lamps supplementing the main headlamps. We had an override or frigg switch to give extra control to the right hand fog lamp, so that it could continue to shine on the edge of the road, which was often bumpy with potholes. The French roads could be notoriously rough! We all resisted the temptation to put all the lamps on against an irate yellow lamped car; for we respected that we were visitors to their country and thought that they could be jealous anyway. Our lights were quite capable of burning the paint off the boot of the car in front!

So on down the tree lined route, (it was Napoleon who planted these to give shade to his troops) skirting south of the Principality of Luxembourg to Metz and the German border at Saarbrucken. I had been asleep, lulled by the drumming of the car and the road, so when things went quiet, I woke up to the sound of German speech; we had reached the border. It was 5.30am and still dark and there was very little traffic about, so with the minimal of formalities we proceeded into town, through the traffic lights all flashing yellow, as a warning to proceed with caution, and passed the street cleaning vehicles spraying everything with water. Looking for the way to Karlsruhe and the crossing of the river Rhein (Rhine), we spied an all night petrol station, so filled up. We had managed to cross France without having to pay their high fuel prices. (The French did not have to pay road tax!)

Dawn broke and we were surprised to find an establishment offering breakfast that early, particularly as we were in the northern part of the Black Forest. None of us were impressed by the black German bread, but enjoyed the coffee. Nevertheless, suitably refreshed, we continued down to Stuttgart and the autobahn to Munchen (Munich). There were no open road speed limits on most of the continent then, so we were well aware that a car in the rear view mirror a far distance behind could be travelling at twice our speed, and we were not hanging about anyway! We arrived at Munchen at lunchtime and we were very pleased to be well on schedule having covered the 860miles from Stafford in 24hrs. It was an education to be part of that city traffic. Everyone, but us, knew where they were going whilst the patience of the German car driver is well known – 'Definition of a microsecond? - The time between the traffic lights turning green and the car behind blowing it's horn!' At one set of traffic lights, (not just flashing yellow now that it was daytime) I was driving, and I was a little worried when a pedestrian waved me forward six inches to line up properly like a racing grid, six cars in a row, but with only five lanes the other side!

We kept heading southeast on the A8 autobahn to Salzburg and the land of 'The Sound of Music'. The traffic was now very heavy, but of course it was Friday afternoon, and as we approached the Austrian border, the 60mph traffic jam eventually stopped. We thought that there must have been a big accident, for it was the first major hold up that we had. After a time of creeping along, we eventually came to some police cars where their officers were questioning many of the car drivers in the hold up. We had not realised that this weekend was the start of the Salzburg music festival, so along with some other traffic, we were diverted through some minor woodland roads and into Austria avoiding the area around Salzburg.

We had intended to stop that evening for a nights sleep, as we had been travelling for nearly thirty hours, including the ferry, and had covered about a thousand miles! However, we opted to continue on into the Alps along good but twisty roads; (for no motorway had been built then) for a few miles and then look for a *gasthoff*.

It was very much the case of "no room at the inn", for 'Full' signs etc. were displayed everywhere; so we persevered onward up into the mountains and as we were starting to wonder if we would ever get a bed, we spied a *restaurant/gasthoff* and enquired, or rather Ian did in his one year of schoolboy German (I am sure that his teacher would have been very proud). They could make us a meal but no rooms were available, but they sent us to a village where they said we should be ok. We carried on along the road some three or four miles before turning off on to a dirt track towards the village. We found the "Gasthoff" suggested to us and rang the big old cowbell hanging at the front. Dusk was now falling and we could see and smell the smoke from the wooden fires in the chalet type houses on the side of the mountain. There was a big pile of logs stacked up all round this chalet, a sure sign that it could get very cold. Eventually the door was opened by, 'the witch out of Hansel and Grettal'. She was wearing the typical Austrian dress of a flared and layered grey and black skirt, white blouse and pinafore. Her grey hair was tied up into a bun and complimented by small national health type spectacles perched on her pointed nose. Her thin face had that weathered look common to those people who live and work out in the more severe climates of this world.

We were now getting desperate and decided to investigate. Ian's schoolboy German came into use again. She guided us up a wooden staircase to a landing from which a door led into a large dormitory with about ten beds in it. The beds were again wooden sided holding a basic mattress and covered with a continental quilt, the first one that I had ever seen. On a table were a bowl and a large jug full of water so we could have a wash; the bathroom we presumed. The toilet however was at the other end of the corridor and consisted of a hole cut into a plank of wood at seat height. Because the chalet was built on the side of the mountain this toilet was actually three stories up. The original long drop, to the common midden shared with the cattle and goats in their apartments under the whole place.

Well we were 'three tough young men' on our travels and out to experience the different cultures of the world! However, it was not the place to take ones girlfriend.

It was now dark so we decided to stay, but the witch did not understand that we would like a meal, so we left our cases to show that we meant it and returned to the *restaurant/gasthoff* for our meal. Not understanding the menu, we opted for the same as the adjacent table, for their dinner certainly smelt good. It was a kind of Hungarian goulash, but I am sure that by this time we would have eaten anything. On returning to our chalet we were met again by the witch. When Ian mentioned the word beer (even I understood that bit of German) she gave us her first smile and quickly ushered us into the parlour where she indicated that we should sit down on a wooden bench by a large rough-hewn refectory type pine table. At the end of the table was sat a wizened old man in his rocking chair, wooden of course, and next to him a slightly younger version of him. A neighbour we found out later. At the kitchen side was a big log fire crackling away with almost a sense of laughter at our trepidation. The one side of the fire fed into the 'original' range of some sort of oven and hot plate but with an arm sticking out holding a pot on a chain over the fire.

Three large litre sized pewter steins were plonked in front of us and filled up with ale from a jug, home made ale I presumed, which continually made the rounds topping up all our steins. It is amazing that after a few sips of ale how the conversation improves, and this was no exception and it did not seem to matter that only a smattering of the German language got us through the evening. I gave a cigarette to Ian and the old man was intrigued by the packet, took hold of it, and then took a cigarette out and put it behind his ear, even though he was still smoking his own, and then gave one to his friend. Still it all made for an interesting evening. We now had the problem of persuading madam witch that we would like breakfast in the morning. With great hilarity, using empty eggshells, from off her sink and pointing to an ancient cuckoo clock on the wall, we thought we had got the message over. However we were a bit concerned with what she was now cooking for supper on the old range. Slices off a large sausage containing, we dare not wonder, for it smelt a sickly sweet smell and could have been some poor lost traveller who had refused to pay up!

We were all pleased that we had returned to the other restaurant for our evening meal!

We did not remember what time we managed to get to bed but all slept remarkably well. Duly refreshed, we went down to the parlour for breakfast in the morning. We were truly amazed to be served with fresh baked bread, slices of ham and cheese along with perfectly cooked boiled eggs, and supplemented with home made jam and lashings of fresh coffee. After the hearty breakfast came time to pay up and say goodbye to the old couple whom we had at last warmed to. We gave the old man some of our English cigarettes and he was absolutely delighted. Also, we discovered on filling in the visitor's book, that the previous guests had been there in June. Now this was the time of year when the old couple should have reaped some reward from the tourist trade but being realistic I am sure that not many people would have put up with a *gasthoff* with no running water!

We wanted a picture of our now friendly witch, so Bunny coaxed her outside of the chalet by holding on to the bill with some Austrian shillings until we were all outside. The old man suddenly appeared with some of his home made cigarettes as a present to us which we 'gratefully' received and we were most surprised to be given a parting hug by both of the old couple. I didn't think that they had many visitors at all, and now that it was properly light we could only see about a half dozen chalets in total in the little hamlet, which was also on a no through road. So at last we departed soon after 9am and headed ever deeper into the high mountains southward towards Villach.

Chapter 3

The Alps and Southward

There were four main passes that we needed to cross on our journey over the Alps and we unanimously decided that each driver would tackle one. The first, the Pass Lueg, I had driven the previous evening, but had been a bit disappointed in that, although spectacular, it was mainly a twisty road through a gorge. No high pass on that occasion, so the others agreed that I should do the last pass instead of drawing lots as originally intended.

The spectacular vista of the mountains kept opening up as we climbed through the vast forested areas, which explained why everything was made of wood. We got the impression that we were just climbing forever. The poor car felt that it had lost most of its power, but it was the continual uphill route that we had to negotiate that sapped it's energy. Today there is a motorway directly from Salzburg to Villach, which tunnels under the highest alpine peaks, but in 1966 we had to take the narrow twisty road up and over the Radstadter Tauern at some 1738 meters (about 5700ft). The traffic was quite heavy so quite a bit of overtaking was necessary, usually done straight after a corner when visibility was good and the other vehicle was in the wrong gear! When we approached the dirt road section we were well into a thunderstorm with heavy rain lashing the car and impromptu streams crossing our route. The crash of thunder and flashes of lightning seemed to add to the whole scenario of the mountains. It certainly had a humbling effect on all of us. The road then suddenly dropped down into the valley below and I was sure that the views would have been spectacular too, if we could have seen them, had it not been for the cloud.

With a driver change we were soon climbing again, up the Katschberg at only 1641 meters. The rain had eased a lot and as we went over the summit, the breaks in the clouds gave us stunning views, particularly southward, and we suspected that the sun was shining down there. I was particularly impressed by these mountains and promised myself to return some day when I would have time to explore. Our mission was though, to catch that plane on Monday night! The long descent all the way to Villach in the south of Austria brought more speed to the little car, making up some of the lost time on the steep ascents. It was a very beautiful part of the world, with the mountains, forests and some lakes all making up a moving picture postcard on our journey. The mainly chalet-type houses were not cramped together but were scattered almost haphazardly over the countryside. From Villach we took the road to Klagenfurt and passed by a lovely long lake, The Worther See, set in the woods. We were surprised that so many people were swimming and sunbathing there, until we realised it was Saturday. We had nearly lost all track of time, and of course now that we had left the storms behind, the temperature was warming up.

From Klagenfurt we headed due south for the Yugoslavian border and on to Ljubljana, the first major town of yet another country. But first we had to cross the fourth of the main passes over the Alps. This, the Loibl pass, was not a well used route, for most traffic that did actually want to go into Yugoslavia, usually went from Italy or from much further east where the mountains were less severe. I had taken over the wheel and enjoyed the fairly good road, which climbed up into the Lloibl Mountains. The scenery was starting to become quite breathtaking and the little Imp had to work quite hard as well, as we kept climbing higher and higher up the pass. Suddenly there appeared a junction in the road, to the right the signpost said 'Tunnel', and to the left it said 'Summit'. As I started to turn left on to a gravel track the other two shouted "to the Summit" so who was I to argue? They had just confirmed my decision. This lovely dirt road, which we later found out, was often used on some of the major international car rallies of that era. It twisted and wound its way ever upward and at a wonderful hairpin bend, we decided to stop for lunch. The weather was by now just perfect, with an occasional white fluffy cloud to break up the deep blue sky. I shall never forget the views back into Austria and the panorama of the high Alps which, even in August, had some snow glistening in the sunlight. It was all just so magnificent. We lunched on some bread, butter and cheese, which we had bought from a village on the way and supplemented this with a tin of corn beef that Ian, as catering manager, had brought from England!

After taking some photos of Bunny driving round the hairpins, we continued on up the track. At one point the road just seemed to cling to the cliff face as it still kept climbing and then suddenly we arrived at the Summit of this lovely pass. The area at the top was relatively flat and comprised of a small car park, a wooden office type building, evidently the customs post, and the barrier across the road. There were two cars parked up, one right by the building, and the other by a safety fence on the edge of the precipice. As we got out of the car a tall immaculately uniformed customs official approached us and warmly greeted us with, in perfect English, "Good afternoon gentlemen, would you like your passports stamped as a souvenir? And have you come to look at the view?" We chatted away but he was not really expecting us to carry on over the pass into Yugoslavia. Most traffic that did arrive at the customs post in the sky just collected a souvenir stamp and the little traffic crossing the border went through the tunnel. We would soon find out why!

We were now at about 7000 ft. higher than any of us had ever been. This fourth pass was certainly 'La piece de la resistance'. We went to the safety fence and peered down at the road, or rather goat track, dropping steeply down and hugging close to the mountainside before disappearing from sight into no mans land, for the Yugoslavian customs post was a few miles away near to the exit from the tunnel. I was still driving, and after all we were all rally drivers weren't we? It's only a bit of a mountain road! So the barrier was raised and I gingerly crept off the summit trying not to notice the steep hill sign showing 33%! The car of course was still quite heavily laden, so I felt caution was the operative word. The road or track did not appear to have been maintained for years; with potholes and water gullies littering the route. In a couple of places even part of the road had fallen down the mountain and some of the concrete blocks, usually familiar on any mountain road on the continent, had disappeared also. Yes if we thought that the route up the Loibl was hairy, this was absolutely awesome. In fact, a year or so later the summit road was closed for safety reasons! As we descended, we then entered the tree line zone again, and now there was the added problem of vegetation also over the road, but we succeeded without mishap and arrived at the Yugoslavian border crossing point. How very different to the Austrian side!

Since leaving the Austrian customs post, we had actually been in no man's land, for now in front of us was the Yugoslavian border control where it's coils of barbed wire stretched into the woods on either side. Across the road a barrier of a round pole, painted in red and white separated us from two soldiers with machine guns held at the ready! Tatty wooden buildings completed the customs post, along with a basic sentry box wooden shelter adjacent to the operating end of the pole. The post's kaki coloured jeep type car and an MZ motorcycle were parked next to the buildings. Two uniformed men were looking at a rough looking lorry with local number plates. Whilst one seemed to be examining papers the other was looking under the tarpaulin covering the back of the truck. The whole scene could have been taken straight out of a Second World War film.

The officer finished with the papers belonging to the lorry driver and pointed to him to move the truck over to a parking area, and then signalled the one soldier to open the barrier for us. I nervously drove forward until the officer signalled me to stop and signed for us all to get out of the car. Evidently the local driver would have to wait as they now had three foreigners to question. There were no other visiting vehicles in the compound and the barrier was then lowered back to its normal position. The officer looked long and hard at each of our British passports and carefully examined the visa stamped in each of our books before signing us to follow him to the open door of the first building. A sign over the door seemed to imply that this was the customs post, and the three of us stood silently out side. I could see the officer showing the passports to another man and then we were all relieved when the three passports were stamped with the customs logo over the corner of the official visa stamp. We were very pleased that we had already obtained the visas from the Yugoslavian Embassy before our departure from England. The officer returned to each of us individually our own passport and with just a hint of a smile waved us towards a second barrier on the road out of the compound. This pole lifted as I slowly drove forward and on to the road out of the customs compound. We all were quite relieved to have come through smoothly in about thirty minutes. As we drove away I half expected to hear the crackling of machine gun fire behind us.

In a few miles, as we lost altitude, we joined the main road from the Italian border which is the most common route into Yugoslavia and headed down to Llubljana. Yes we were now behind the iron curtain and going ever deeper into this communist country.

President Tito was the man in charge and, even though having responsibilities to Moscow, ran his country in a more moderate way than others in the communist block. I doubt that we would have had such an easy time at a Russian customs post. However, as we drove on, leaving the Alps behind us, the late afternoon sun and a rumbling stomach reminded us to be on the lookout for a restaurant or at least somewhere to get a meal. We were about fifty miles short of Zagreb where we thought that we should find food, so we pushed on down the main road, which was in surprisingly good condition.

On the outskirts of Zagreb we found a modern motel and campsite, which was in complete contrast to everything else around and eagerly entered the restaurant to enjoy a good meal. The place was quite full, mainly of truck drivers, but with a smattering of German and Italian tourists. We had just finished a hearty meal of tender rump steak, or was it ox? When a late middle-aged couple came up to us, they were Scottish and ours were the first English voices that they had heard on their two weeks journey from Athens. They were absolutely amazed when they learned that we had a plane to catch from Athens in just over forty-eight hours. They inferred that we would never do it as the state of the roads increasingly deteriorated the further into the country one went. They also warned us, like the people in Ian's book, about traffic with poor lights and horse drawn carts with none! The Scottish couple just would not travel at night themselves. So with wishes of good luck, full tanks of petrol and satisfied by a good meal, we set off searching out the main motorway from Zagreb to Beograd (Belgrade).

It was about 8pm and getting dark when we quite easily found the autoput or Yugoslavian motorway. Now this road had been built by the Germans at the time of the second world war for troop movements and was basically a single carriageway concrete road running relatively straight to Belgrade. The first part of about twenty miles or so had been resurfaced with tarmac, and was not in too bad a condition, but we soon ran on to the continuous drumming concrete road. It had been laid in slabs so the constant knack as the tyres also changed level at the next slab sounded like a train clanking over the rails on its track. Only a few of these cracks had been filled in with pitch or tarmac and many other parts of the road had been repaired using even more concrete, but there were many, many untended potholes which shook the car about and which could even cause us to lose control. It was even worse than the minor French roads with all their potholes and parvee. I tried to relax and eventually slept with the monotonous sounds of the road hypnotising me into slumber. It had been a long day and it was my turn to rest as we were still keeping to the plan of regular driver changes. Two to three hours during the day, but about two hours at night, for we had no long, even meal stops until Athens tomorrow evening.

Why does something always happen when I am asleep? Well the screech of tyres, the sound of horns and the realisation that we were travelling on the so-called grass verge was enough to wake anybody up. We had survived, but survived what, I wanted to know. The normally calm pair of Bunny and Ian excitedly explained the situation, and we were very lucky. The traffic was thinning out with just a few wagons trundling along the 'motorway', but it was the situation of poor vehicle lighting that had nearly led to our demise. We had often seen trucks with just one headlamp working; however what Bunny had met were two trucks, each with only one headlamp, running side by side, one overtaking the other, and filling the whole of the road. On approaching them they had just looked like one lorry! Yes we were very fortunate and understood why the Scottish couple would not travel at night. We had no choice if we were to catch the plane from Athens, so we determined that the navigator should also keep a sharp lookout instead of cat napping, as is usual on an easy navigational section. We were right to do that as we also encountered horse drawn carts and even an ox cart all without lights and on the 'motorway' too. Nevertheless we made it into Beograd (Belgrade) having followed the Sava river valley all the way from Zagreb and actually covered the two hundred and fifty miles in four hours, not bad under those conditions. We were nicely on schedule.

Now Beograd is the capital city of Yugoslavia and it is at the point where the Sava River joins the mighty Danube. Having been used to only British rivers, it was indeed difficult for us all to appreciate the big continental rivers. We could only imagine the size of it and thought of the spectacle when the river was full of alpine melt water in the springtime. Whilst I appreciate that it was midnight and very dark and we could not see the Danube, any notions of the romance of this river conjured up from the music of its birth country Austria were quickly dispelled by the austere and drab buildings on the streets as we made our way to locate the second part of the autoput heading south to Skopje. There was very little traffic, just an occasional car, always black in colour, scurrying guiltily away into the shadows of the dimly lit streets. So, we started to hunt for signs to Skopje and for fuel as well.

Just when we began to wonder if the official state map, showing the petrol stations, was in fact true, we spotted the bright lights of the state owned petrol company's filling station shining out like a Christmas tree, and headed straight for it. There were no other cars on the forecourt apart from our trusty steed and as Bunny endeavoured to make sure of getting the highest-octane grade of petrol possible, (no choice only petrol or diesel) the attendant appeared. It was obvious that he had just been awoken from his sleep and he grumpily indicated to us that this was not a self serve station, grabbed the fuel nozzle from Bunny and proceeded, against Ian's protesting in a few words of German, to go to the back of the car and would have, I am sure, stuck it up any orifice he could find! I doubted if he had ever seen a Hillman Imp car before and he probably thought we were German lads, because of Ian's language. Some of his countrymen still had bias against the Germans because of their occupation during the war. However, when he saw the GB plate on the back of the car he brightened up and let us show him the fuel tanks under the 'bonnet' where the engine should be! He was even more confused when we wanted to fill up the second tank!

At last we were again full of fuel, some fifteen gallons, and ready to head off through the night to Skopje some two hundred and seventy five miles away, with another one hundred miles or so to the Greek border. We succumbed to the temptation of some coffee from the oldest vending machine we had ever seen, and ventured to ask the attendant, by showing him the map, the way to the 'motorway' to Skopje. We were the only customer he had whilst we were there, and as he happily directed us off the forecourt gesticulating in a generally southern direction the car clock said 1.00am. However somehow we took the wrong or old road to Skopje, but nevertheless it ran approximately parallel to the autoput.

After a few miles, still looking out for carts and lorries without lights, we came across a diversion, which seemed to have been there for a long time but we had no choice but to take it. The road still headed south but it was a minor one, we were still however travelling onwards. Not so surprisingly we found another diversion. A diversion on a diversion, and even though we had reasonable maps, they are not as good as the British Ordnance Survey maps, which we were more used to. We appeared to be now heading in the wrong direction; the middle of the night; a communist country; an inadequate map and no signposts. All this added up to the danger of getting lost and into trouble. I later learnt that whilst Bunny was driving he hit a large hare but with minimal damage to the car, I expected that the hare would end up in some locals cooking pot. At a cross roads we spotted, for all three of us were now awake, a diversion sign stuck by a tree and followed it (not the tree). The tarmac had now disappeared but the track was quite good and seemed to have been well used. On entering a village we were surprised, but should not have been, to be confronted by two large wooden cable drums, some six feet high, in the middle of the road and a trench, containing the electric cable from the drum, stretching away down the track we wanted. No barriers or lights in evidence either. Still, as there was plenty of room to the side, and we could even see tyre tracks from lorries, we continued on through the village. There was no one about. Not even an ox cart!

It didn't seem long however until we were surprised to regain the concrete autoput, still full of pot holes and bumps, and turned southeast towards Skopje on our way to the Greek border. I had been fortunate to travel extensively in England and Wales and so had got to the point of just enjoying the different situations that travel throws at one. So an attitude of 'expect the unexpected' was part of my philosophy, brought on no doubt by the rallying culture! I was interested now to see a rare signpost to Sofija in Bulgaria and realised that our route took us close to that border as well. (Sofija was the start of some of the long distance endurance rallies of the late fifties and early sixties. How they managed with the customs system I just didn't know).

As we entered the town of Nis, we were all astounded by the large crowds of people everywhere. Not just adults or youngsters (as can be seen today coming out of the late clubs and bars of a city) but people of all ages, men, women and children, old and young just milling around. It was quite disconcerting at first, as up to now, we had not seen more than a handful of locals gathered together at a time, in the daylight or evening. However the time was approaching 4am and we could just not understand it! They did seem quite friendly though, and we were glad of that as the crowds were all over the roads, but there was no other traffic about anyway! Many times the car was brought to a standstill by the sheer volume of people, but I patiently kept creeping forward with inquisitive locals almost pressing their faces against the car windows to get a better look at its occupants.

They were, as equally intrigued by our maps and us, as we were of them. Because it was quite warm my driver's window was open, so a couple of times, when stationary, I pointed out the name of their town, Nis, on the now illuminated camera route guide. This caused great excitement and Ian also showed people our route through Yugoslavia and onward to Athens. So they knew what we were about, but we never found out what they were doing. But it was early Sunday morning!

Another two hours, and one hundred and twenty five miles motoring, brought us to where many people had lost their lives in the recent cataclysmic earthquake at Skopje. It all seemed very quiet now; I wonder if that was what the crowd was doing at Nis? But there was no sign of damage there. However the road veered west towards Skopje and we actually turned left before the town and headed south towards the border one hundred miles or so away. In the half-light of dawn we could pick out another river valley, which we would vaguely follow until the Aegean coast. We would be well into Greece by then!

Close to the Yugo/Greece border near Gevgelija, we stopped for breakfast at a nice motel come restaurant standing on a hillock over-looking the river valley and enjoyed good food, paid for with the last of our Yugoslavian dinars, and had a brief rest. We were certainly to be glad of that breakfast later! The three of us were again intrigued by the horse drawn carts, which for the first time now we were able to see in daylight. Most were four wheeled and shod with rubber tyres with a large flat bed trailer to carry the produce. But this Sunday morning, the trailers were packed with men, women and children all off somewhere important, I presume. Did the people of a communist country go to church then? The sun was shining and the prospects were for a lovely sunny day and so with fresh fuel also in the car, we were all in high spirits as we approached the border.

This customs post looked newer that the one at the Loibl, but was still manned by soldiers with machine guns. We were relieved to receive a going out stamp neatly matching the previous one and were cleared through in about ten minutes or so. Ian now informed us that our time through Yugoslavia and distance covered meant that our average speed through the country was actually higher than the maximum speed limit of Yugoslavia! It was a good job that we had entered and departed on two consecutive days!

Chapter 4

Greek Bureaucracy

At 8.00am on Sunday the 7th August 1966, the car rolled forward on to the 'Stop' sign outside the Greek customs post and came to a halt. The scene was in strict contrast to the Yugoslavian posts. The newly painted buildings glistened white in the early morning sun and an odd assortment of vehicles were haphazardly parked on the paved area adjacent to the customs building. There were two Greek soldiers, one by the entrance to the offices and the other by the barrier. They stood smartly, in the military "at ease" stance, dressed in traditional costume of elaborate black tunic over a white shirt, and with the knee length flared skirts to compliment the long socks and black shoes of the outfit. The whole theatre was finalised by the rifle with fixed bayonet being held in one hand with the butt of the rifle by the soldier's foot. They looked much more impressive than any photos that I had previously seen of the Greek military, and certainly did not look effeminate. We remembered warnings about taking pictures of any military establishment so kept our cameras out of sight.

A thin tanned man in his thirties sauntered out from the door of the customs office and beckoned us to pull over to the side of the building. We all got out of the car, and with our passports in our hands approached the official. He looked briefly at the passports and looked bewildered, so went back to the doorway, said a few words in a language we could not understand, and returned with an older man similarly dressed in white shirt and grey/white trousers. Was this the customs uniform? They evidently were not very used to having English cars coming out of Yugoslavia to see them! They were very interested in the car, probably had never seen a Hillman Imp before and were very confused by the engine being situated in the back of the car. I was sure that they thought we were importing a spare engine. They were also equally interested in the two petrol tanks at the front, never seen twin tanked cars before either! They looked again in the boot and under the bonnet and inside the car so that I was sure we would have to remove our luggage from the roof rack for inspection.

The two officers then indicated for us to follow them into the office. Seated in the middle of three chairs behind a long desk was evidently their boss, a portly man of about fifty years of age, with the normal white shirt showing sweat stains. He was sweating profusely and asked to see our passports. Even though it was only about 9am on the car's clock, the temperature was steadily rising: we were in for a warm day but we didn't know how warm! He looked at each passport thoroughly and then with a sigh got up and ambled out to look at the car. We went through the same rigmarole as with the two other officers. The engine in the back again causing trouble! But he still didn't ask to see under the canvas sheet covering our suitcases on the roof rack. After some time, probably prompted by the sun rising higher and getting hotter, we all went back into the office and the three customs officers sat down behind the table in their relative hierarchy and each lit up a cigarette. The boss man proceeded to fill out a form. Something was happening. Ian whispered, "be patient lads" and proceeded to offer me a cigarette. They stopped us. They could smoke but not us! We should have remembered that.

After starting on a second form, the younger officer was sent outside to the car. I noticed that he wrote down the registration number and also I presumed the make and model of the car as it took him quite a long time. On returning, the information was entered on to one of the forms. They then wanted something else but we didn't know what. Suddenly I thought about the car tax disc on the windscreen. Two of them came out with us and I pointed out the tax disc. No it was not that, or perhaps they didn't know what that was! But then Ian thought about the car registration or log book and produced that from his document case. Good old Ian, they liked that but could not read the English, but we could not read Greek anyway! However by pointing out the registration number and Bunny's name, Andrew Todd on the logbook and showing them his name in his passport they seemed happy and proceeded to fill out more forms. Evidently a mistake must have been made on one.

So another form was made out, passed to the boss man for his signature and passed to the third officer for the all important rubber stamp. And this went on and on. One piece of paper was completed, signed, stamped and then thrown into the waste paper basket along with the incorrect forms. We were unaware that, that piece of paper was the very piece that we would need later! So at long last with smiles and handshakes we climbed back in the car and headed south towards Thessaloniki (Thessalonica). We had been there some two and a half hours. It was a good job that they were not as busy as the Dover port authority!

It was not long before the road turned to a motorway and we were glad of the opportunity of making up some of the lost time. On arriving at a tollbooth, which we were not expecting, we tried to determine the cost in Greek drachma; most signs were in conventional as well as the Greek alphabet. The booth operator accepted a British ten-shilling note for payment, but I don't think we got a good rate of exchange, but we were happy and at least were not in the situation of being done on the amount of change given for a large denomination note. It was certainly getting warmer and as we had never experienced hot climates before, we wondered how hot could it get? And so, the little car purred on south through Macedonia, the birthplace of Alexander the Great. We were now certainly travelling in a land of history and different cultures.

We were all greatly amused by following a car, which had obviously been rolled over in an accident, crabbing along with wheels completely out of line and its body all twisted. It looked as if the damage was old, but even so the car was full of children as well as mum and dad! Yes it was a steady reminder that, like Yugoslavia, no compulsory car insurance operated in Greece, so it was an added incentive to be cautious, and yet we had nearly four hundred miles to cover between the border and the city of Athens, where we wanted to be encamped at that evening! Traffic was light but we were also reminded about the national green buses which, being a law unto themselves, have priority over all other traffic, (I think that they also carried the post, like the post buses do in Switzerland). The sound of their claxon horns blaring away on a mountain road is something I shall never forget.

Nearing the Aegean Sea not far from the port of Thessaloniki, there was a road junction, which brought home to the three of us, the scale of our undertaking this journey. The road from the north forked left and right, with the west and east road forming the third side of a triangle. In this triangle a wooden road sign for Istanbuli (Istanbul), pointed to the East and Athinai (Athens) to the West. Certainly an international signpost if there was ever was one, and not to be confused with the contrived finger post signs sometimes seen at airports etc. In a little while, the road veered south again and we were delighted to be now running alongside the Aegean Sea from time to time. Strange it seemed to us were the pine forests lying to our right on the hills near to the coast. I normally thought of pine forests with a colder climate, but nature is never that logical, as we would find out more and more on our travels.

At the town of Larissa, we went due south and up into the Greek mountains, instead of following the coast road, and on to Lamia where the two ways met. The first part was relatively straight across the coastal plain, but then we started climbing and the road deteriorated into a typical twisty mountain track. Although tarmac, it was covered in a layer of gravel brought down off the hills by wind and rain. It got hotter and even hotter, until the speed of the car was forced down to about thirty miles per hour in order to avoid the engine from over heating. We even propped open the rear bonnet to help with airflow, but that didn't help much. We stopped to allow the car and ourselves to cool down a bit, but there was just so little shade up in those hills. We scraped together some lunch from the bits and pieces we had left over but he biggest problem was fluids, for our bottles of water purchased at breakfast time were getting depleted. I searched the landscape but there was still no sign of life at all. We had not even seen a dog or goat, never mind any people for a couple of hours or so; and the sun was only just over its zenith. We carried on slowly, so as to not over-heat the car, finding that it was cooler with all the windows closed to keep out the hot wind! It was very uncomfortable and fatigue was starting to set in. We had been on the road for a long time.

"Is it a mirage or is that a building up ahead?" exclaimed Bunny, in a rare outburst of emotion. As we drew nearer, we were so pleased that it was some form of café or taverna, but it was miles from anywhere. Outside, were an old green bus, (probably lost) a couple of battered cars and a moped: but no people. Ian spotted a crate of empty coke cola bottles by the entrance doorway. Grabbing one of these, the normally reserved Ian charged inside holding the empty bottle aloft in one hand and three fingers aloft on the other. (I was glad there was three of us and not two!) Now the barman could have given us three empty bottles, but he showed compassion for the three mad English men out in the mid day sun, it was too hot even for a mad dog. He directed us to a table and produced three ice cold cokes from his fridge along with three glasses of water. They were the best coke cola I had ever tasted and I thought of the film "Ice cold in Alex" about men trapped in the desert. We decided to get a snack and some spare drinks and water to take with us and issuing thanks we departed much to the amusement of the few locals sheltering from the sun in the relative comfort of the old taverna.

We dropped down from the hills to Lamia and wrong slotted briefly before picking up the main coast road to Athena. (Athens) [The combination of two alphabets, combined with a different spelling of the same town in different parts of the country caused difficulty to anyone, never mind three very tired British lads]. It was certainly stunning scenery. However, a combination of the temperature and the long journey meant that we all just wanted to get to the transfer flat in Athens. (I will explain more about this flat later). Those last few miles just seemed to drag on indefinitely. Eventually we realised that we were in Athens itself. Not a signpost or a welcome to Athens banner could be seen, but I suppose that we were just in the outskirts of the city.

It was 5pm and a fresh driver was needed - yours truly again. We had been warned about the high density of traffic and the vague sign posting, with most of it being in the Greek alphabet anyway, so we all needed to be on high alert. If we had thought that Munich was difficult then Athens was horrendous. The high melting point tarmac caused tyre squeal by the traffic on all corners, with those green buses making the most noise. When I left half a cars length from the car in front, then not just a taxi, but also a bus pushed in! We soon noticed that there were very few undamaged cars in the city, and of course again, everyone else knew where they were going! However eventually, we got to our destination. We had made it! The little Hillman Imp, thanks to Bunny's expert preparation, had completed the nearly 2300 miles without a hitch in about 76 hours from leaving Stafford. Quite an achievement, especially as much of the journey was on difficult roads. I understand that now, one can travel the whole way by motorway, but that would be cheating!

The transfer flat was located in the old part of the city close to the area known as 'The Plarca', where the old commercial centre of Athens was situated, and lies at the foot of the Parthenon on which the famous Acropolis stands. A view of this greeted me on looking out of the window the following morning. I am afraid that is all of the cultural tour of Athena that I am able to give you, for as you will see, the shortage of time for sightseeing meant that I was unable to visit any archaeological sites.

Now, my cousin Carola Morgan and her husband John were involved with a holiday company 'Murison Small', through whom we obtained the plane tickets for our onward journey to Nairobi. They specialised in chalet holidays, normally skiing in the Alps, but also had some chalets or villas on a couple of the Greek Islands. Staff employed by the company stayed at the flat whilst waiting for transport between England and the Islands. They had kindly offered that a friendly face, in that distant city might be able to help us, particularly in getting the formalities sorted with the Greek authorities over putting the car into a customs pound so that the owner Andrew (Bunny) Todd could temporarily leave the country without it. We all greatly appreciated that help and particularly Dave, from the flat, who spoke excellent Greek and who was to be an absolute Godsend to us the following day. The two outgoing Scottish girls at the flat were expecting us. That was a nice surprise and they told us that Dave would be back later and would help us in the morning. They also said that if we didn't mind sharing a room, with one of us sleeping on the floor on a mattress, then we could stop the night at the flat, instead of having to find a hotel, which we had expected to do.

After a shower, a wonderful shower, we wondered out into the evening to find a drink and some food. It was still very hot even though it was now dusk and the various landmarks were being lit up by floodlight. Close by the flat was a bar with just two small tables balanced precariously on the uneven pavement. We sat down wanting an ice cold beer to celebrate our achievement, so were perplexed by the waitress bringing us three glasses of cold water and then taking our order. The word beer has an international connotation and fortunately for us three ice-cold lager beers of the local brew appeared quickly. They tasted like sweet nectar but didn't last too long, but then Ian sussed out the custom of providing a glass of water as a token of their hospitality, very welcome particularly at such a hot time.

A teenage girl, who was probably the daughter of the waitress, as most Greek eating establishments are family owned, appeared also dressed in the uniform of a waitress, and asked us in pretty good English if we had just arrived in Athena? I thought that she had been sent out to see us by her parents after they heard us speaking English. I was still amazed that most people thought of the three of us as being German or Dutch until they heard us speak. I am sure that we didn't look too German, but I suppose that not many British people travelled extensively in Europe compared to other continentals!

She told us that we had arrived in the middle of a heat wave and that the temperature had reached 43°C (108°F) in Athena, but that it had been even higher up in the mountains. Unfortunately some deaths had occurred through heat exhaustion and dehydration. She did not know that we had travelled down through the mountains by car. No wonder that our progress had been so slow. She asked if we would like to eat and said it was cooler inside the little taverna. How could we refuse such hospitality? Any way, none of us were in the mood to go searching around the restaurants or nightlife of the city. Some food and another beer would be all that we wanted before finding our beds. We enjoyed a simple but tasty meal in the clean, although quite spartan restaurant. We thanked our hosts, and then retired back to the flat and bed. I seemed to have hardly slept. It remained hot all night and we didn't need any bedclothes either. Perhaps it was the thoughts of our journey and the venturing into the unknown lands of Africa that held my mind so active. Besides being so tired from our travels, I discovered in the morning that Bunny and Ian also had a sleepless night. We had breakfast at the same little taverna, before meeting up with Dave, whom we followed in his car to the customs offices to sort out the formalities. We could then have the day sightseeing in the city before catching the aeroplane at midnight for the final leg of our journey to Nairobi.

What optimism; but we were young and relatively naïve to the Greek bureaucracy. At the offices Dave explained to them exactly what we wanted to do and we were passed from one department to another. Dave told us just to be very patient! Eventually, we seemed to have the correct department and a young customs man, still dressed like his counter parts at the border, took us all and both cars to the pound. It was a bombsite on the back of an industrial estate next to a compound surrounded by barbed wire. He assured Dave that this was the official customs pound. Now it may have been the official overspill area, but it was not the official customs pound. He now stated that the pound was full up! This was exactly what we had been warned about and had been told by John Morgan, *"under no circumstances agree to leave the car in an area like that"*. Most of, if not the entire car would be missing when we returned! If no pound was available, then some registered garages would park the car safely, but of course it would cost us more money.

Eventually the customs officer agreed to arrange that with his superiors, so back we all trooped to the offices a couple of miles away. The whole scenario was explained by Dave and the young customs man to his boss, who could have been the twin brother of the boss man at the border crossing. I had developed the theory that the hierarchy depended on the portliness of the official, in that in a hot climate the boss would get the junior to do the running about and consequently got very little exercise himself. So we again produced the paper work from the Yugo/Greek border along with Bunny's passport in order to countermand the stamp in his passport of his importing a car. They searched our forms and made out other ones and got more and more aerated. "Patience" said Dave again, "they always get excited". Again we were stopped from smoking, even though practically all the customs officers smoked continuously. (Cheap or confiscated cigarettes I presumed).

Now I didn't understand any of the arguments and reasoning that Dave was so ably putting on our behalf, but I did understand that things were not well. Something was certainly wrong with the papers from the border control. Poor Bunny was getting very worried as all the gestures were directed at him. I thought that he was worried about spending the next month in a Greek jail! At the same time, Ian and I clicked as to what was wrong! We needed the form that had been signed and stamped by the customs people at the border and which had been accidentally thrown into that waist bin nearly four hundred miles away. Surely there was a duplicate, there seemed to be for everything else. No, the one bit of paper they wanted was not at hand.

Ian suggested driving back to get it, but I thought that they might have emptied the waist bin by now, certainly would have with our luck!

Surely, there must be a way round this problem. Dave again explained to the boss man that we had to catch a plane at midnight. Those customs men, at the airport won't let Mr Todd leave the country without his car they emphatically said. You others can go but not Mr Todd! Even Dave was losing his patience and asked to see the headman in order to sort this out. He has gone to lunch they said. "We are now closed, it is lunchtime". So we said we would come back after lunch, "At what time we asked?" "Tomorrow" they said, "We are only here in the mornings!" We all begged and pleaded our case of catching the plane that night but all to no avail, and so we all left the customs offices in a very despondent mood. Dave was very apologetic, but it was certainly not his fault, we would definitely have got nowhere at all without him. It was now time for a conference and to plan new tactics, and the best place to do that is with a coffee in the shade of a pavement café.

Whilst walking along, to a background of incessant tyre squeal, to a nearby coffee house on a cross roads, our thoughts were disrupted by the sound of a crash near to the cafe. There was not too much damage on either car and remarkably no one was hurt, but the accident did partly block the road. Both drivers got out and were arguing about whose fault it was. Our despondent mood was lightened by the antics of the crowd of witnesses who were arguing with each other and every one got so excited by it all. The other traffic blew their horns and some pushed through the crowd and past the damaged cars to continue on their trip. A bus even pushed one of the cars out of the way! So we went and had a coffee at the adjacent café and were all amused to see the two drivers from the accident trying to sort things out over a coffee, whilst the ever growing crowd of witnesses were getting even more excited.

The staff, at the Air France office in Athens, were very helpful and understanding. They were used to the idiosyncrasies of Greek Bureaucracy and said that they could rebook our flights for later. This was certainly a relief, for we had begun to wonder if we would ever get out of Greece. The problem was that there were not so many flights as nowadays, and the next available flight was three days away, with only two seats! It would be a week before we could all travel out together. We decided that Bunny should certainly have one of us to help with the customs fiasco and that one of us should go on out to Nairobi to inform Frank and his parents of what was happening; i.e. that the car won't fit on the plane. We could not phone through to them and a telegram would have taken a week or so, even if it got there. I offered to go on out alone and this would hopefully give the two lads a chance to see Athens; assuming of course that the lost bit of paper could be duplicated. We all felt a lot better and again thanked Dave as he left to carry on with his work.

We returned to the flat for a siesta and relaxed for a little while. The two girls from the flat were going to the beach, for, according to the locals, the best time to go is when the heat of the day is past and the sun is less likely to burn. We eagerly accepted their invite and the five of us squeezed into the faithful Imp. We spent an enjoyable time catching some rays, as a prelude to the tropical sun, and having our backs rubbed with sun tan oil. I would have liked to have had a little swim, but I thought that the water was not very clean. Too near a big city and seaport for me.

The Plarca as mentioned earlier, is the old commercial centre of Athena and boasts many restaurants and tavernas. So, we all enjoyed the company and good food at one recommended by the girls who accepted our invitation to join us. All spent a pleasant evening, before I was taken on to the airport lying to the south side of the city. After checking in at the Air France flight desk, we said our goodbyes and I went through to the departure lounge with "See you and Frank in three days time we hope!" ringing in my ears.

Chapter 5

Two Flights.

I sat in the window seat looking out into the darkness of the airfield, away from the lights of the airport buildings. Beside me there were two empty seats! I do admit to being a little apprehensive being on my own now but it was also the first time that I had flown in a proper aircraft (not counting a Tiger moth, but that is another story) nevertheless I was looking forward to the flight. About eight hours, non-stop to Kampala in Uganda for breakfast, then less than two hours on to Nairobi. Approximately four thousand miles still to go before meeting up with Frank. I wondered if he would be surprised at my leaving the other two behind in Athens. I doubted it knowing Frank as I did. Nothing seemed to bother him.

I had come through customs very quickly with hardly a look at my passport; a stamp and that was that, so I could not help being cross at all the fiasco over Bunny not being able to leave the country without his car! I am sure that if he had been with us nobody would have stopped him from travelling but we will never know. I glanced at my watch showing midnight local time; it seemed as if we would depart punctually. The Air France set up was very efficient and the airhostesses looked very smart in their dark blue skirts, white blouses and scarves all trimmed with red. Similar in style to the staff of the BOAC (British Overseas Airways Corporation: now British Airways). However I was amused by the girls speaking American with a French accent, it sounded very unusual, to me anyway.

I was interrupted whilst deep in thought with all these things, by one of the attractive hostesses who wanted to confirm about my friends not travelling with me. I briefly explained why and I was then asked if I would mind moving, so that a family of three could sit together. She promised that I would have a good seat. I collected my small day bag and jacket and the African family who now would occupy our seats thanked me profusely. The airhostess, guided me down the plane to the middle seat next to a white girl, and then smiled and suggested that since we were both travelling alone we would be company for each other. My new companion was quite petite, pretty with shoulder length brunette hair emphasising her tanned face. It didn't take long for me to realize that she was French and a student, but spoke very little English. Unusual for a French girl, but then I could not speak French either. Oh why did I not take more notice of Mr. Doyle my French master from school? I was always interested in the science lessons rather than languages, if only I had known!

The Boeing 707 plane soon took off, (it was probably the biggest passenger plane at that time) and at last we were on our way heading south over the Mediterranean Sea towards Africa, eventually cruising at 40,000 ft and at about 500 mph. My new acquaintance was very pleasant and with our very limited vocabulary, I did discover that she had come from Paris and was travelling on to Dar-es-Salaam in Tanganyika (now Tanzania) and that her name was Michéle. I tried to explain that I, and two friends, had driven to Athens from England and I was going to Nairobi. I gathered that she was confused as to where my friends were, but I could not explain in French. If we had both been able to speak fluently then that information would have been divulged in a few minutes. As it was, we both laughed as we tried to understand each other and the time passed by very quickly until the stewardesses brought around drinks followed by blankets and pillows for those passengers who wanted them. The cabin lights were dimmed and most people tried to sleep. At least the temperature was civilised, even a little on the cool side, hence the blankets. After having a very hot night in Athens I soon dropped off to sleep.

I awoke with cramp in my shoulder caused by Michéle. She had started off with her pillow against the window but had obviously turned over and now slept with my shoulder as a pillow. Who was I to complain? Perhaps it was French culture. Anyway I didn't disturb her sleep, for she had got an even longer journey than I. I looked up through a roof or round window at the stars. (I have never seen a ceiling window in a plane since). The multitude of stars seemed enlarged and distorted by the glass, but I was amazed at the vast number of them. They could be seen very clearly, no pollution up there! Then I tried to sleep again; if Bunny and Ian had been with me I would not have had a French girl asleep on my shoulder! I felt very happy and contented and dropped off to sleep with thoughts of the wonders of Africa.

Suddenly everyone on the plane woke up with a start, and had that sinking feeling as the plane dropped a few hundred feet! It probably only lasted a couple of seconds. The lights came on and the pilot assured his passengers that all was ok. We had entered an air pocket (or lack of air to be more exact) and these phenomena could exist over the desert in areas of a tropical storm. A storm with no rain, this was new to me. We were advised to fasten our seat belts as it could happen again. It did happen again but not as severe, or perhaps we were just expecting it. Michéle had now a double shock, being awoken by the plane dropping and then realising that she had been asleep on my shoulder. She seemed a little embarrassed by the latter after she had recovered from the former shock. I just smiled reassuringly that everything was all right and she relaxed again. Obviously not French culture to sleep on the shoulder of a stranger.

The lights were dimmed yet again and most people tried to sleep. On looking out of the side window, I was fascinated by the effect of the bright moonlight on the ground. It appeared as if the plane was skimming over a gigantic beach and the moonlight accentuated the vast sand dunes and hills, making them look like the ripples on the sand at the seaside.

I must have nodded off to sleep, for when I awoke, dawn had broken and we were being served with drinks of tea and coffee etc. We would soon have breakfast in Uganda. I could tell that the aircraft was on its long decent on the approach to Kampala but I was most impressed by my first glimpse of the large inland sea, or really the Lake Victoria, the source of the White Nile. (That has and is still the subject of much debate because of the vast tracts of seasonal wetlands to the north and east). This vast lake borders Uganda, Rwanda, Burundi, Tanzania and, of course, Kenya: my final destination. The plane banked low over the edge of the lake and I could see many wild animals running, having been startled by the noise of the engines and the sight of a gigantic silver bird bearing down on them. Then there was the 'runway'. A single strip of tarmac just laid out through the bush, which had only been partially levelled. As we touched down and the four big jet engines went into reverse thrust to help slow the plane as it sped down the runway, the wings seemed to slowly flap as the plane went up and down following the rise and fall of the tarmac. It was quite disconcerting.

We were allowed to disembark from the plane to go the restaurant for breakfast, and for anything else that we might wish to purchase, although I was mystified as to what one was able to obtain in such a place. I stood up and waited in the aisle for my new acquaintance to proceed, like an English gentleman should do, but by the time I had descended the boarding steps to the tarmac apron in front of the airport building, I was very much at the rear of the throng dashing to the doorway of the restaurant and facilities! I thought that I was the only English person travelling on that flight, and realised that the art of patience and queuing is confined to Britain! Whilst every one was pushing to get into the building I took stock of Kampala Airport.

I didn't know what to expect. There appeared to be no fencing around the airport, just a single runway disappearing into the bush. To the side of the buildings, three small aircraft were parked haphazardly. Two of them having what I thought was the Ugandan flag painted on the fuselage, perhaps this was *the* air-force as those two planes looked like old fighter planes, whilst the third plane seemed to be a small passenger one. So the 707 certainly dwarfed the surroundings and looked completely out of place in that location.

The main single story building to one side at the end of the runway, housed the restaurant and a basic shop, with a few souvenirs for any visitors who had forgotten to buy presents. The one end of the building extended upwards for a second story, the observation tower a must for any airfield! Eventually I managed to get into the café, for that was what it really was, and I was attracted by Michelle waiving at me from a table by a window at the end of the room. She had been there before and knew the score! My 'friend' had collected two breakfasts from a kind of self service counter all laid on by Air France. So croissants etc, with a large pot of coffee went down very well and I decided that air travel on my own was not too bad at all! My thoughts turned to an old school friend, a compatriot of mine in the swimming team, Frank Goodwin, whose parents had lived and worked in Kampala during the 1950s, and I wondered if they had ever returned? Frank seemed to be a popular name in colonial Africa!

An hour and a half later the big plane roared down the undulating runway and with a final burst of speed launched itself off one of the crests and we were airborne once again and heading on my last leg of the journey to Nairobi less than two hours away. Those two hours just flew by, as I tried drastically to improve on my very limited French vocabulary!

It was mid morning when we landed at Nairobi airport where I, with a number of other passengers disembarked from the plane. I said *au revoir* to my travelling companion and was surprised but nevertheless delighted to receive a hug and a kiss on both cheeks in the true French tradition. After collecting my case, which arrived quite quickly, and being quizzed by the immigration police, I wandered into the entrance lobby of the arrival/departure area of the airport. It was somewhat bigger than that of Kampala.

Frank Rothera called me and greeted me with a handshake and asked about the journey. Perhaps he never noticed that Bunny and Ian were not with me! Or more than likely, was just waiting for me to explain what had happened; never flustered or unduly excited like a true English man! We walked out of the airport into the sunshine of Kenya. Well one does expect the sun to shine in the tropics! It was just like a nice hot summer day back in England, (when we actually had them) and not the oppressive heat that we had experienced in Greece. Frank reminded me that Nairobi lies at about 5500 ft (1680 meters) and about 90 miles south of the Equator. But it could get very hot and as we would ultimately find out, in some parts of our travels it would become extremely hot. An interesting fact about aircraft landing at Nairobi is that normal cabin pressure is set to the equivalent of 5000 ft as an optimum balance of air pressure, and being less air than say at sea level, one becomes tired on a long flight, but the altitude at Nairobi is higher, and therefore less oxygen than in the aircraft! Some acclimatisation would be needed.

Frank's father, David Rothera, had kindly arranged to keep his older standard black Volkswagen Beetle for our use when he had part exchanged it for a Volkswagen 1500, and thanks must be given to the garage as well, for I am sure that they would not have realised the amount of, and type of use, that the poor Beetle would have to endure! As we exited the airport on the main Mombasa road towards Nairobi, I noticed that the land opposite the airport was quite well fenced and with much higher than normal fencing. This was the Nairobi National Park which is perhaps the smallest, but easiest to get to, game park in Africa. As we drove from the airport the some five to six miles into town, it was so very strange to be actually driving back on the left hand side of the road, a legacy left over from British colonial rule in East Africa. Yes it did seem so strange, after 2000 miles on the right hand side on the continent of Europe, to be back on the left, some 7500 miles from home.

I was astounded by the amount of luxuriant vegetation in Nairobi itself; a complete contrast to the quite dry and arid area around the airport. We drove along a tree lined avenue with its abundance of exotic flora like the beautiful bougainvillea, with its deep pink and brilliant red hues bringing a welcome splash of colour to compliment the blossoming jacaranda. Some of the main roads and streets in town were similarly clothed and it all gave the impression that Nairobi had been built in a natural forest.

As Frank's parents were both working that day, we went for some lunch at the Thorn Tree hostelry annexed to the New Stanley Hotel in the centre of town. Only the best for Frank, or in his words, 'that is the only place to have ones first meal in Kenya'. It was a large open-air restaurant situated at one side right on the pavement, with much shade provided by a massive thorn tree in the middle, from which the establishment got its name. As would be expected with the best hotel in town, the furnishings and layout were tastefully done with the other side of the room merging with the reception area and bar of the hotel. We enjoyed a delicious roast beef luncheon with all the trimmings expected at a good hotel in England, along with a glass of Tusker Ale, the locally brewed German style beer. We were also served attentively by local waiters looking very smart in their white tunic type jackets and black trousers.

Over the meal I told Frank about the problems with the Greek customs and that Bunny and Ian should be with us on Thursday morning all being well! We chatted about the journey and about what we would be doing during our stay in Kenya, and about some of the conventions that were expected of us. Younger men whilst in town often wore shorts but not long shorts, which were reserved for older men. Both were expected to wear long socks with shoes or boots and not plimsoles (trainers). Even the natives were expected to wear respectable dress, for there was a bye law which stated that the only men allowed on the streets of Nairobi without trousers, were the Masai, and no one could fully control them.

Frank drew my attention to the bar area, which now looked like a scene out of a movie. Two elegantly dressed middle-aged American women were talking to two Safari guides, who looked like the traditional white hunters. The one I am sure doubled for John Wayne in the big game film 'Hatari', or perhaps he was John Wayne himself. The other was slightly shorter and quite thin; I thought he must be the tracker of the duo. Both their complexions showed the harsh reality of being out in the bush with the sun and wind blowing the red scorched earth in their faces. I noticed that both carried sheaf knives and a handgun neatly kept in its holster by their side. It was said about the Thorn Tree, like the 'Café de Paris' in Paris, that if one waits long enough you will see someone interesting.

We completed our leisurely lunch with lashings of coffee, eagerly served to us by the waiters, from a bottomless pot, coffee is a staple crop of Kenya. We made our way northwards towards the village of Kiambu, and through the shantytown, a haphazard conglomeration of huts and shelters, some even constructed with corrugated iron sheeting, inhabited by many locals from the countryside trying to eke out a living in Nairobi. The countryside we were now travelling through was again a contrast, for this area is known as the White Highlands and is even today the main farming and estates community of Kenya, if not of the whole of East Africa.

The Rotheras lived about twenty miles out of Nairobi on the edge of a coffee plantation, and much to the liking of Frank, if not us all, on a dirt road. We had lost the full or normal width of tarmac road, when we turned off the main Thika road towards Kiambu. The carriageway then became a single-track tarmac road but with plenty of room either side. No problem you might think, for when two vehicles met, both just pulled over with two wheels left on the tarmac and two on the dirt! Well! There were two problems; firstly, many drivers do not want to pull over, why? because of the second problem. Often there is a drop, (we found one about two feet) where the rains and traffic erode the surface away! So the driver needed to be brave and very observant. After Kiambu the track was all dirt road, hard packed and quite level although very dusty. The surface was serrated as if running over corrugated iron, so the drumming sound made was quite disturbing until one got used to it.

The large red roofed bungalow which the Rothera's rented from the plantation farmer (they had sold their house intending to move to South Africa in a couple of years), lay in about two acres of grounds and was approached up a curved drive from the gateway on the road. The whole site was surrounded by a high thick hedge and trees, which were essential for reducing the amount of dust blowing from the dirt roads on to the bungalow and its grounds. At the back of the bungalow were some outbuildings and adjacent to these were two independent breezeblock dwellings in which lived the houseboy and the gardener with his family. The houseboy used to go home to his family on a regular basis, and whilst I thought that this accommodation was very basic, I soon learned that it actually was good to what some local families enjoyed. I was introduced to these local Kikuyu people and shook hands with each, along the Swahili greeting "jambo" (hello) in the formal polite manner, as is the custom in East Africa.

During the evening the conversation with Frank and his parents, after wondering what our two friends were up to in Athens, turned to Nairobi and how it all came about. Prior to the turn of the twentieth century the city of Nairobi did not even exist. A quote from *'The Genesis of Kenya Colony'* sums up the location nicely:

'A bleak, swampy stretch of soggy landscape, wind swept, devoid of human habitation of any kind, the resort of thousands of wild animals of every species. The only evidence of the occasional presence of human kind was the old caravan track skirting the bog like plain'.

"So how did the modern city get here for it seems well established?" I asked. It was all because of the railway, which started from the coast at Mombasa and arrived at Nairobi in mid-1899. (I will discuss this 'Lunatic Line railway' later in our story) The Masai, a nomadic and intensely proud people, brought their beloved cattle to this place, known as *Enkarre Nairobi* meaning 'Place of Cool Waters', where a small river that ran through the area brought fresh water from the hills to the North West. The whole area was populated by a vast assortment of wildlife including the 'big five' game which most people think about in East Africa, lion, rhino, elephant, leopard and buffalo along with giraffe and a multitude of other grazers. Deadly snakes, and insects like the mosquito and tsetse fly were also endemic. What an inhospitable land.

Despite all of this, it was thought that Nairobi was the best location for a resting place and inland depot for the railway. It was now too far to be served from Mombasa and the land onward to Lake Victoria was indeed very difficult to cross! So a shantytown quickly sprung up around the rail depot and in 1907, over five years from the completion of the railway, Nairobi became the administrative centre for the newly created East Africa Protectorate, covering the modern countries of Uganda, Kenya and Tanganyika (Tanzania). An outbreak of plague caused big problems, but the authorities burnt down part of the infected shantytown to stop the spread of the disease, and this paved the way for the town to grow into the modern capital and economic centre for East Africa. Kenya gained independence from British rule in 1963 and had Jomo Kenyatta as its first leader or prime minister; with Kenya still playing an active part as a member of the British Commonwealth. *(During the last forty years the development has changed Nairobi out of all proportion to the city as it was in 1966).*

Everyone realised that I needed some sleep; as it had been nearly a week since I had had a good nights rest! When I awoke next morning, I was surprised to find that it was nearly midday, but after a belated breakfast I felt ready to explore. First, we had to wait for Bunny and Ian to catch up with us in Nairobi! So, it was in fact the following morning that saw Frank and myself at the airport trying to gleam information about the arrival time of the flight from Athens. (We assumed that there could be only one flight out per day max.) Nobody but nobody knew anything, there was just no flight that day – but perhaps the airport didn't know there should be one!

So in desperation, Frank managed to get hold of his father who, because of his connections, knew the guys in air traffic control – they should know what aircraft are about?! David Rothera said that he would follow it up, but information was slow getting through, so suggested that we report back to him in the afternoon. Having watched air traffic control in action with its comparative light trafficking, and having explored the airport, we found ourselves talking to a couple of British RAF lads. They offered to show us around their aeroplane. We had noticed a large RAF plane sitting on the tarmac to the side of the maintenance buildings with two of its four engines missing. For years these contraprop-engined aircraft were excellent for reconnaissance search and rescue operations because of their ability to travel slowly over vast distances between refuelling.

Yes the Shackleton certainly looked from a bygone age of aviation, but it was nonetheless impressive. The plane was one of two being used to observe the blockade of Rhodesia, by the Wilson British government, because of the UDI (Unilateral Declaration of Independence) by their Prime Minister Ian Smith. So as the RAF lads had only got one spare engine and had trouble with two, they were enjoying the sunshine whilst waiting for spares. They had been waiting for six weeks already! Frank and I spent a happy hour or so being shown around the plane, provided that we did not tell anyone about it. (I would think after forty years it's ok to speak of it now!) Then we left to see if any more information had materialized about flights from Athens. The problem was we were now the wrong side of the customs and immigration boundary and the gate, which we had gone through with our RAF friends, was now locked.

Frank has always had an air of confidence, so through the maintenance hanger we walked as if we owned the place, well Frank anyway, with me following as inconspicuously as possible and not even having got my knees brown yet! We eventually found ourselves in the admin offices where Frank continued to try to find out where the Athens plane had got too. Perhaps tomorrow they said, so as the sun was accelerating its journey to the west and out of sight, we decided that as no more planes were due to land that night; we might as well go home. It is interesting that there is really no dusk or dawn in the tropics, for there exists approximately twelve hours of daylight and twelve hours of darkness and the transition between the two is very quick.

That evening David Rothera informed us that the flight from Athens had been delayed at Cairo in northern Egypt, reason unknown. But those passengers for different destinations were being accommodated on alternative routes and so our two friends should be at Nairobi tomorrow morning. So next morning after calling in town to buy myself some safari boots, which I had been very impressed with over the last two days, Frank and I again found ourselves out at the airport. Eventually after lunch, an old aircraft droned overhead and landed haphazardly on the runway, then very slowly taxied to a place on the apron by the arrivals lounge. We could hardly believe what we were seeing, for it was like a scene from the 1940's; for the plane was a twin engine Dakota supporting an unknown national flag. "Here come Bunny and Ian," joked Frank, but never a truer word was said in jest, for among the few passengers who disembarked, were our two friends carrying their own luggage! With no hold ups at immigration and customs, who I was sure felt sorry for the passengers; Bunny and Ian were soon with us in the airport lounge. With a rare display of emotion, we all hugged each other with a genuine brotherly affection, for I know that we all at some time wondered if we would ever meet up in Kenya.

During the evening the belated travellers recounted their story after I had left them at Athens airport. The next morning after seeing half a dozen officials they actually managed to see a senior executive of the Greek customs department who sorted out the fiasco by the next day. The offices still only opened in the mornings, so they had the afternoons to themselves. After servicing the car in the street, Bunny and Ian also sampled the cultural aspects of Athens with a tour of the Acropolis and enjoyed a breathtaking 'son èt lumiére', in English at the Parthenon, also managing to visit 'the Odeon of Herodes Atticus' and the 'Theatre of Dionyses' near to the Acropolis Stadium. The car was properly garaged at a main dealership near to the flat and sealed by the customs a few hours before their flight out in the early hours of Thursday. They expected to be in Kenya Thursday afternoon.

They met a Greek family whilst on the beach and were invited back to their home for a meal the following evening. This was all because three girls who wanted to learn English were greatly amused at Ian's antics of trying to sell packets of tea since his wallet was left in the flat! They both certainly had a very enjoyable evening. Ian, who as catering manager, had brought out some packets of English Typhoo tea, gave these packets as a thank you gift to their new Greek friends, who were absolutely delighted, as such luxuries were just not available in Greece. A very pleasant contrast to the bureaucracy experienced in getting the car properly garaged.

However, Bunny and Ian eventually left Athens at 0130hrs Thursday, on an American Douglas Corporation DC6 propeller engine aircraft. The Ethiopian Airways organisation decided to stop at Cairo, and so after a few hours, they continued their exploration of North East Africa, in the dark. Stopping at Asmera in Eritrea bordering the coast of the Red Sea, they experienced further delays. They again had to leave the plane and even though still night time it was very hot and sticky. Facilities were very basic to non-existent, and they were dumfounded to have to pay a tip to the toilet attendant to use a filthy fly infested hole in the ground. Having no local currency, Bunny in his infinite wisdom suggested that Ian should give him some of the local home made cigarettes that we had been given by the old man during our nights stay in Austria. Neither Ian nor myself liked them very much but were too polite to say as such to the old man. But the toilet attendant was jubilant, probably the best tip he had ever received! Eventually the plane took off again and after an 'interesting' flight they landed at Addis Ababa, in the Abyssinian or Ethiopian Highlands for refuelling and another investigation of the local facilities.

They were ushered out to another waiting plane (a DC3), but thought that it only had two engines and still being dark could not tell what it was. No one could speak English to answer their questions but at least they could talk to each other! They boarded the Ethiopian Airways Dakota; probably left in the Sudan at the end of the Second World War, and headed south in daylight. A long bumpy flight saw them arriving, with great relief at Nairobi. It had been a long haul with difficult travelling and they were also an extra 24hrs hours behind schedule, they were very thirsty, hungry and tired, but happy to be united with Frank and myself. To think that during my journey, I had to endure the company of a pretty French girl who had the audacity to fall asleep on my shoulder! At long last, we four musketeers had completed the first part of our mission to actually get out to East Africa and we all wondered what adventures were in store for us during our exploration of Kenya.

End of part one.

Sunco Safari Photo Album

The Alps

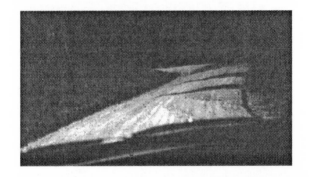

Loibl Summit.   Outward Journey

**Horse & Trailer
Southern Yugoslavia**

Cultural Athens

Entrance to Nairobi Game Park

Stay in Your Car !

Tree Tops   **Tea Party Guest!**

John on Equator

Ian at Thomson's Falls

Fourteen Falls

Bunny on Good Dirt road

Dust!

Roadside Vendors

Lunatic Express

Above
Hells Gate

Fischer's
Column

68

Longonot Summit

**Dr. Livingstone
I presume?**

**Masai
Herdsman**

Dug Out Boat

Mombasa

Sunco Studios

John, Frank & Andrew with Elephant's Foot. 2006.

Part Two

Kenya

Sunco Safari
Location Maps

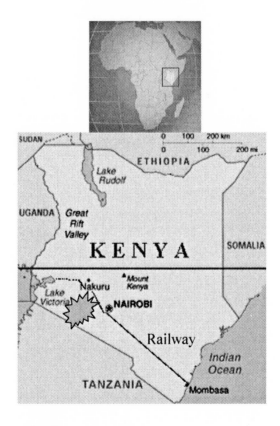

 **Rift Valley
Exploration**

Map of Our Rift Valley Explorations

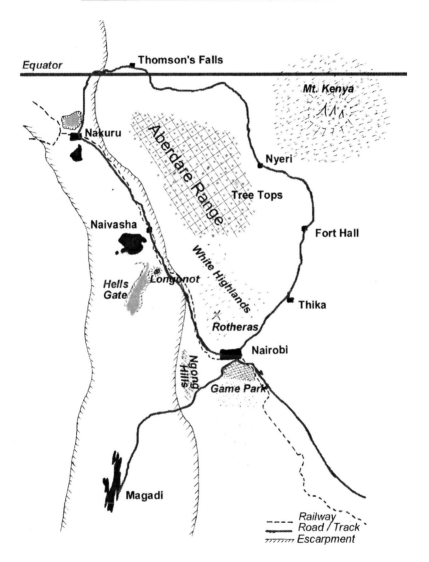

Chapter 6

Nairobi National Game Park

The main gate of the game park was most imposing. A steeply ridged red tiled roof arose from the single story buildings on either side of the driveway, while the centre part of the roof stretched up to bridge the entrance to the reserve. Cream walls were enhanced with stone buttresses and neat windows to give the whole structure a very modern appearance. Actually, there was no gate at all, just a giant cattle grid sunk into the road beneath the tunnel like effect of the buildings. The high fence bordering part of the western and north western, side of the park stretched away into the distance. In practice this fence did not cover more than a few miles and it appeared to have been put up as a token gesture of protection. To protect 'whom' from 'what' I wondered, as game parks are there to try to protect and conserve the wildlife of the country. The city though did need protection, predominately from large predators, as we had already heard stories of big cats surprising people in town. It was not uncommon for a leopard to be found roaming the streets looking for dogs and recently one was discovered in the kitchen of a house in the suburbs. This all added to the mystery and adventure of 'going on safari'. So we rumbled over the old railway lines used in the cattle grid and on into the courtyard. The ticket information office, supplied basic maps and a guide as to what we might expect to see but we were advised to stay in the car except at a couple of designated places. I wondered why it may be ok to alight from the car in one place but not another. I was sure that the animals could roam anywhere!

It was suggested that a good place to start would be the orphanage, which was also used as a veterinary hospital. This seemed strange because in the wild the normal law of the jungle existed and the dramatic theatre of the hunter and the hunted was constantly being played out. However the issue of conservation was now very much at the forefront on the agenda of the authorities and National Game Parks. Until the start of the twentieth century the area around Nairobi and of course the vast tracts of savannah lands, from Sub-Sahara Africa to Cape Town, were inhabited by a seemingly endless supply of many types of animals.

Not only the well-known big predators but also the larger grazers roamed the land along with many varieties of their smaller cousins, in an ecological balance carefully maintained over thousands of years. The co-existence of the native peoples with the wild animals had also found its natural balance, for though there were instances of domestic animals being picked off by some predator or other there was a close relationship between the people and the wild beasts. The Masai, Somali and Kikuyu herdsmen, amongst others, often had a few honorary livestock from the grazing multitudes mingling with their own long horned yet usually scrawny looking cattle, with which a mans wealth and status was judged. So as these traditional nomadic inhabitants of this vast land coaxed their herds along ancient migratory routes in search of better grasslands, produced by the seasonal rains, they harmonised with the thousands of wild animals all seemingly inter-reliant on each other.

It is true that the natives killed animals for their own use, wild ones as well as their own domesticated ones, which supplied food, hides, clothing and shelter for their tribes. They also killed predators, which might attack them or their herds, but generally each had that respect for the other. The herdsmen had that ancient built in love and respect for nature, in all its awesome creation and it was said that a Masai youth could not become a man until he had singly killed a lion! Very few modern peoples could survive in that magnificent though hostile environment. The wild animals too, seemed to be able to co-exist, generally accepting the wanderings of the Masai, perhaps now the most common of the nomadic and other peoples, but certainly well aware of the sharp spear, arrow or stone if they were to encroach too close to the village or cattle. The Masai built traditional mud huts with grass roofs, which were usually grouped together and surrounded by a token hedge or boma made from branches of the notorious thorn tree. The sharp barb type thorns could shred all but the very toughest of skins and hides so were a good protection from marauding creatures particularly at night.

With the advent of the railway from Mombasa to Uganda and the birth of Nairobi as the administrative centre of the British control in East Africa, the whole area was opened up to an epidemic of tourism, namely the 'Big Game Hunter' whose sole intention seemed to be to collect as many trophies as possible. Among those who poured into the country armed with rifles was the former United States president, Theodore Roosevelt, who in 1909 wanted to collect natural history specimens for the museums back home. His entourage of six hundred porters and professional big game hunters killed over five hundred animals, the trophies and skins from which found their way back to the States. At that time the visit of Edward, the British Prince of Wales, also helped to popularise the big game safaris. The result was astounding; the carnage equivalent to genocide, as there could be no comparison to the accuracy and devastation of the bullet compared to the bow and arrow or spear.

The growth of Nairobi also meant restricting the free movement of all animals as the migratory herds and their followers were unable to travel along some of their ancestral routes. During the 1930's Archie Ritchie, a game warden, and Mervyn Cowie spoke out for the protection of these indigenous animals and petitioned the colonial authorities about the setting up of a national park to help reduce, even if not able to stop altogether, the wanton destruction of these magnificent creatures. The advent of the Second World War delayed the negotiations and brought on the additional problem of the animals getting too used to the many soldiers working and training in the area around Nairobi, to the extent that some could turn into man eaters! However on December 16th 1946 the then governor of Kenya, Sir Philip Mitchell signed the inauguration of the first park in East Africa,

'The Nairobi National Park'.

Nairobi National Park is perhaps the smallest game park in Africa, being approximately 45 square miles, but that does not detract from the fact, considered by many, for it to be an ecological masterpiece. In the western side of the park, the higher rainfall encourages forest, including the Cape chestnut and the beautiful Croton, along with all the wildlife that such a profusion of trees will support. The eastern and southern parts portray the extensive plains, valleys and ridges, which with about half the rainfall of the forest environment, produce classic savannah grasslands dotted with several types of trees including acacias of many varieties, the arrow poison tree and of course the ever prolific thorn tree. The northern edge of the park, the Empakasi Plain, is separated from the city of Nairobi by a fence. However the boundary on the southern side is basically a gorge fed by numerous rivers with the vast area south of the river, although not the actual park, being the Kitengela Game Conservation Area, which stretches down to Kilimanjaro and the Tanzania border.

Although the orphanage did have quite a number of young animals, many of which were looked after until they were ready to be re-released back into the wild, there were some adults as well. I was surprised to see a camel (or was it a dromedary?) that did seem to be a very long way from its home, normally associated with North Africa and desert conditions. A pair of young cheetahs, sprawled lazily in their enclosure, eyed us suspiciously, and then the low deep growl of a lion drew our attention. The old male had a fantastic black tipped mane and reminded me of 'Clarence' the old cross-eyed lion featured in *'Daktari'* a popular TV African wildlife series of the early sixties. Lions have a strict social type of existence. The head of the pride has the responsibility of looking after his lionesses and their cubs, which are all his, from other marauding males wanting to take over his pride. Lionesses are renowned for their hunting ability and usually work in groups and the whole pride benefit from a kill, although each member must take its turn in feeding, for the hierarchy is strictly adhered to.

This old male, which we were looking at, had finally been driven away from his pride. The battle scars were evident and he would have been killed if he had not run away. Unfortunately old age made it difficult for him to hunt and he consequently survived by scavenging, which was the reason why he was found looking for easier prey in the suburbs of Nairobi. He was so well known to the game wardens that he had been given the chance to live out the rest of his life in peace. Little did we realize that he was to be the only lion that we saw whilst visiting Kenya. A large lone chimpanzee caused us all much amusement with his antics; he was methodically demolishing his own house or sleeping shelter and then breaking up the wood into smaller pieces. Evidently it was a kind of game played with the wardens who had built him several houses!

So armed with maps, information and cameras instead of rifles, we four intrepid hunters climbed back into the black Volkswagen Beetle and trundled off on our first safari. On leaving the compound we were amazed and also a little apprehensive as we passed a giant skull and crossbones. The large elephant skull with its accompanied crossed femurs was certainly a warning emphasised by the sign

'Stay in Your Car'!

Now Frank had of course previously visited the Nairobi National Park, so Bunny, Ian and I hoped that he would know where to go. It was not long before we saw various types of antelope, the impala were quite pretty in the dainty way they searched for choice morsels of grass, but we were all impressed by the majestic horns of the males. This was a first reminder that even the most innocuous looking animals can soon cause someone harm, particularly if cornered or protecting their young. The eland the biggest of the antelope family and the size of an average pony sported a pair of very sharp horns. Its jumping ability certainly helped it to survive against the big cats and other predators. If it wasn't for the horns it could have been mistaken for a wild ox. It was however the Thomson's gazelles, or 'Tommies' which were one of my favourites. Although quite small they had the ability to run, jump and turn in a quite remarkable manner, a necessary trait for survival in Africa. The rich brown colour contrasted with a black stripe along their flank and the twin horns sported by both males and females certainly put these beautiful animals in a class of their own. As we rounded a corner between the trees on the edge of the forest, I remember a silent gasp on sighting my first giraffe. They certainly looked tall and I had not yet seen the big male who was to appear from around a copse of acacia. The giraffes that I had previously seen at Dudley or Chester Zoo were pygmies compared to the size of this magnificent creature, which I now beheld. This was to be one of those memories that would stick in my mind for the rest of my life. No wonder that the authorities had arranged for the telegraph poles to be more than twice the height of those back in England!

It was Armand and Michaela Dennis who first brought the world of the Kenyan savannah to the TV screen, in their remarkable filming of many of the wild animals, which we would see in real life on our trips into the park. Yes, we made several trips, for as a thirty-minute film might take many weeks to shoot, likewise we could not hope to see so many different animals on just one visit. I therefore take the liberty of combining some of our experiences from the various safaris, which we made. The one fact that remains paramount is that it was we four, Frank, Bunny, Ian and John who were restricted to a mobile cage, the wild animals were the ones able to roam freely where they wanted to. We saw very little other tourist traffic and sometimes it seemed as if we had the park to ourselves, a blessing perhaps but not so good if we ran into trouble or broke down in the car. The animals of the modern safari parks of Europe are almost domesticated, so those parks cannot compare to the vast areas of the African savannahs. Of course the tremendous work that the specialist parks and zoos do, particularly towards conservation, has thankfully prevented the extinction of some species. So with place names to find from the map, such as: - Lion Corner - Leopard Cliffs - Baboon Escarpment - Hippo Pool - Rhino Drift - and Cheetah Gate, we set off with cameras at the ready in search of big and small game.

It had been a very early start, for dawn had not yet broken, as we again trundled over the cattle grid at the main entrance to the Nairobi National Park at about 6am. The idea of course was to try to see some big cats, as during the heat of the day, like most moggies, they preferred to rest up in the shade and catnap. 'Perhaps today we might see some action!' The remarkable splendour of a large scarlet coloured jewel rising out of the eastern sky heralded the birth of a new day. We desperately tried to align the sunrise with the horns of what I thought was a buffalo nonchalantly standing on a ridge ignoring the spectacular kaleidoscope all around. From pitch black to bright daylight takes just a very few minutes in the tropics so our attempted picture of a lifetime was not to be. The animal was just too far away!

Even though it was the big game that was the main attraction for us all, the amount and variation of bird life was immense, an ornithologists paradise. The giant ostrich, the world's largest living bird and often reaching more than seven feet in height, can certainly run too! One specimen kept up with the car at about 30 mph before veering off into the long dry hay-like grass at the side of the track we were following, and headed towards its friends mingled with a small herd of zebra. A very odd combination I thought, zebra and ostrich but, as I was to learn later, nature has a wonderful way of co-existence. The acute hearing and keen sense of smell of the zebra combine with the sharp eyes of the ostrich to form a mutually advantageous interchange of talents. This cooperation between many species acts as an early warning system to the other, for many predators of all sizes are constantly on the lookout for a meal. A lone thorn tree supplied the infrastructure for the nests of a colony of yellow weaverbirds. The seemingly untidy haphazard clumps of dried grass wedged in the upper branches, were nevertheless intricately woven together by these tiny expert thatchers of grass and small twigs. It was Ian who spotted another bird or rather a few, which seemed to be aimlessly circling high in the deep blue sky. "Buzzards" cried Frank "and there are some vultures as well". That could mean only one thing, a kill! So by following the track and then carefully negotiating the grassland it was not long before we arrived at the macabre site and the squabbling chaos surrounding a hapless zebra.

The cats had gone, probably lion as the carcass was quite a large animal, so we assumed that it had in fact been a night time kill, for many lion hunt at night. We quite nervously got out of the car for a better view, even though we had driven as close to the scene as we could. Nevertheless the car doors were left slightly ajar in case a quick retreat was needed. Frank assured us that the animals were all too engrossed in the kill to worry about us, providing we did not try to steal some of their meat! Three or four hyenas were already at the feast and we all shuddered at the sound of those mighty jaws crunching through bone. They nearly always seemed to be the first scavengers at a kill, although they often will go for unwary or weak prey themselves if the opportunity presents itself.

A couple of jackals skulked in the long grass at the edge of the well-trodden battlefield. One dived forward to grab a piece of meat dropped in an argument between two vultures, then the other darted in to take another morsel from the body, narrowly avoiding the sharp claws and snarling teeth of a hyena whose muzzle was dyed red with blood. We instinctively ducked at the shadow of a vulture coming into land. Although the large wingspan gives this scavenger the ability to soar on the thermal air currents to great heights, when it has decided to land, the exact place it does so, is by way of luck rather than judgement. The formidable talons of its undercarriage seemed to just miss us as it careered into the mob demolishing the carrion. I thought that the vultures really did look ugly with their hooked beaks capable of tearing the flesh off any carcass and the featherless face with the bright red protuberances made me shudder as they fought with each other for another piece of the dead zebra.

Yet there was one character which resembled the undertaker of this theatre of death by parading up and down like a funeral director, with his hands held behind his back as though hidden in the tails of an old fashioned frock coat. Yes, the large marabou stork, with its ten feet wingspan portrayed an aura of evil being both macabre and grotesque in appearance. It waited for the carcass to be pulled apart so that its long beak, with the power of a pickaxe and the grip of long nose pliers, could reach for the succulent parts still left in the body cavity of the zebra. Other large birds namely the buzzards started to come into land, impatient for a piece of the action before the feast was over. The well-fed hyenas looked around at the squawking horde of birds both airborne and on the ground and then looked at us! Not a word was said as we cautiously and silently withdrew to the safety of the car. We had not witnessed the chase but we had seen at close hand the reality of the law of the jungle.

"I wonder where those lions are", said Ian holding his camera at the ready "but to get some really good close up pictures I must have a telephoto lens". We all agreed and Ian vowed to try to get one to fit his dad's Leica as soon as possible. It was then, when we were all engrossed in our cameras, changing film etc: that Frank stopped the car just over a brow as the narrow dirt road twisted and turned over the seemingly endless undulating plain. There before us on the track only a few feet away, without any sign of fear, stood two magnificent leopards. Probably a pair of males, for even though quite thickset and fully grown, they still looked young. When mature, leopards tend to be loners, so were these the cats responsible for the zebra kill? We doubted that, as we were a couple of miles from that scene and we thought that the zebra was a bit too big for them, and often leopard like to take their kill up into a tree for safe keeping. But we may have been wrong. The sight of these two leopards just looking at us four lads in our 'cage' caused us some amusement. A zoo in reverse! Those two great cats then just nonchalantly meandered off into the long grass and we watched them slowly disappear from sight.

Later when we recounted this tale we were told that the cats were probably cheetah as leopard are quite rare and difficult to see. However after having a film developed, we were able to confirm that our sighting was that of leopard. This was certainly a rare privilege, for many local people who have visited the game park many, many times have never seen leopard close up.

It was late morning as the sun climbed higher into the deep blue almost cloudless sky. The temperature was rising too and the inevitable dust stuck to the perspiration pouring from our bodies. We tasted the fine powder continually and it got everywhere. You just could not get away from it. The dust was carried on the breeze from a dust cloud caused by and which obliterated a small herd of unknown creatures. Perhaps wildebeest, or gnu as they are more popularly called, for they always seem to be associated with herds and dust to my mind. Frank didn't think so, as it was the wrong time for their migration through the eastern part of the park, but it could have been. We decided not to investigate more closely because of the dust cloud. In any case we would not be able to see much and we didn't want to get cameras and ourselves choked up. 'Nor the car either' inferred Frank as even the special air filters can very soon get clogged up too, an inherent problem of driving in dry and dusty climes. Frank was laughing, a deep mischievous laugh for only he knew what was so funny, to him anyway! "Oh I forgot to tell you, that dirt is the staple diet in Africa: if you don't eat it as dust you eat it as mud! You should see this lot after the rains". Yes, the ground could soon turn to a quagmire of thick glutinous red mud.

Punctures! They seem to be inevitable; the last one had been only a week or so earlier on the M6 soon after our departure from Stafford at the start of our mammoth journey. That seemed like another world, another lifetime, for so much had happened in such a short period of time. Yes, we were still looking for lion but now our car had a puncture. In reality we could have been plagued with flat tyres so we should have been grateful that this was only our second one. Its where they happen that is the inevitability of the problem, the first was on a quite busy stretch of motorway in England where we didn't want much traffic for a blow out and the second was in the middle of nowhere. Well a savannah plain in East Africa, for we had now just passed a sign stating that we were at 'Lion Corner' and it also advised us to 'stay in your car'. Here there was no traffic. We had seen a car in the distance an hour ago, and previous to that a tourist zebra bus. (A Volkswagen Combi-minibus painted in black and white stripes in order to resemble a zebra. I did not think that most animals were taken in by this ploy but the American and German tourists loved them).

There was nobody about at all, so there was nothing else that we could do but fend for ourselves. Ian and I mounted guard on the lookout for lions whilst Frank and Bunny quickly and efficiently changed the faulty wheel as if on a special timed stage of a motor rally. I was sure that now was the time that we would see the lion that we so desperately looked for. We were just about to get on our way again when we were all surprised and amused by a game warden, resplendent in his uniform, who arrived on his regulation bicycle, a trusty black steed made by Raleigh of Nottingham, England. We asked if he knew where the lions might be, and assured him that we were ok, now that we had replaced the flat tyre. The warden directed us over towards the area where the lions were thought to be with the words "well they were there early this morning". Yes that was where the zebra kill had been. With a cheery wave the lonesome game warden trundled off down the dusty bumpy track on his bicycle in the direction of the lion kill! Modern health and safety officials would have had a heart attack, (meals on wheels!). Perhaps though he was from one of the Somali settlements scattered around the southwest part of the park, for these local native peoples lived in co-existence with the natural wildlife, big cats and all.

A place called Hippo Pool, we were told, was certainly worth an investigation. So another fine day saw us tentatively looking down a steep pathway to the river. The gorge had lessened allowing the river to widen out into some quite big pools. The vegetation was very dense around the sides of the river which supplied the much needed water to the trees and other plant life, which in turn supported a great variety of other life. We found it difficult to see, for the pool water was very still and the sun reflected off the surface causing us all to squint. It certainly was a very good location for predators to lurk patiently and wait for some unsuspecting victim. The ancient residents of the great Nile River used to call the hippopotamus, 'great water cows' for they are not a flesh eater, these behemoth creatures are strictly vegetarian.

However a movement on the far bank of the river caught my eye and a large crocodile slid stealthily into the water barely causing a ripple. Unless one was looking no one would have been aware that one of the most efficient predators on this planet had entered the water just below us. I wondered how many of his friends were around as well. We had been warned not to venture down the pathway to the river for more than one or two tourists had failed to return after an encounter with a croc. Hippo too, can be very dangerous even though they don't usually graze on the lush riverside grasses in daylight, for if caught on land they become very frightened and a frightened animal is always very aggressive. I had heard stories about these tremendous one ton creatures meeting someone on one of their narrow paths and understood that they could run at up to 20 mph. Their giant jaws, with 30 inch 'tusks' and the strength of a JCB earth grab bucket, certainly earned great respect from us all. We unanimously agreed that to venture down the river path would be foolhardy.

Just when we had given up hope of seeing some hippopotamus, the water rippled and a pair of nostrils broke the surface followed by another and then a third. The outline of these fascinating giants could be plainly seen even though still covered by an inch or so of river water, and then they surfaced and afforded us a remarkable view of these magnificent creatures. Yes, one of the most lethal of all of Africa's dangerous animals was only a few yards away; we all hoped that they stayed down in the river.

A scream resounded, above the grunting and snorting of hippos in the pool and the chattering of monkeys in the trees behind. We quickly headed back from the edge of the small escarpment to where three vehicles stood on the impromptu car park. Baboons had appeared and they wanted to join in with the picnic which a family were trying to have next to their car. A girl of about twelve got frightened and jumped quickly back into the car but made the fatal mistake of taking her sandwiches with her. The speed and agility with which the monkey got through the open window had to be seen to be believed. The girl went out through the opposite door to be faced by even more baboons awaiting their share of the picnic. Frank charged to our faithful VW and grabbed our lunch to entice the hungry hoards away from the girl. That heroic act succeeded and also brought the grateful girl's parents out of their state of shock. Everyone was more than a bit anxious, for the sight of the baboons with their yellow fangs snarling and scrapping over the bits of food certainly brought home the fact that most wild animals in Africa are very dangerous. Bunny decided to retreat to the safety of the car whilst Ian was trying to take some pictures. I don't know who was most surprised, for when Bunny had settled himself in, he realised that two baboons were also in the car looking for the rest of our lunch!

There was a drive-in open air cinema in Nairobi, or rather on the city's outskirts for it was strategically placed right on the northern edge of the game park. Well, the film showing on one occasion whilst we were there was non other than 'Born Free,' a remarkable film about Elsa one of three abandoned wild lion cubs, found and reared by Joy Adamson, who then encouraged them to go back into the wilderness. Actress Virginia McKenna, who played the part of Joy, and her husband Bill Travers were so concerned with the ecological aspects of the film that they started the charity 'The Born Free Foundation' which still continues today to do tremendous work in the care of big cats the world over. We just had to go and see the film in the setting of the cinema next to a game park. During the film we were sure that the sounds of the roaring of lion were not just those from the soundtrack of the film but those of their live relatives in the game park too. Towards the end of our stay in Kenya we were talking to one of the game wardens about our travels and trips around the area, and we told him that whilst we appreciated that elephant did not normally live in the park we were disappointed to have come all the way to Kenya then not see a lion. The reply: "Still it does not mean however that the lion did not see you"!

86

Chapter 7

The White Highlands

As a complete contrast to the savannah grasslands and forest area of the game park and the adjoining southern plain, the 'White Highlands' region was quite unique in all of Africa, for it's dramatic change of environment. This was the local name given to the geographical area north of Nairobi, which stretched as far as the forests of the Aberdare National Park, whose mountains reached over 13000 ft. The White Highlands were established by early European settlers as the farming and estates centre of the whole of East Africa. The altitude of 7,000 ft to 10,000 ft gave a temperate climate comparatively well watered by the clouds, which mysteriously seem to form in most mountainous regions.

The terrain though was quite accessible. The plateau, even though undulating and with long ridges from which the excess rainfall was nicely drained away, was a maize of roads and tracks. The majority were typical dirt roads maintained by a grader, a tractor type of vehicle with an angled plough blade to remove the bumps and fill in the hollows. In more remote areas a tree was just towed behind the vehicle to sweep and maintain the road for other traffic. Thus the green countryside of the area supported an abundance of arable and of course general farming communities as well. The sight of herds of British traditional and Friesian cattle grazing in a meadow of lush green grass reminded us of the rural farming back home in England on a beautiful summers day. Pig and poultry farming were also popular along with sisal, maize, corn and other cash crops. However the biggest income came from the coffee and tea plantations.

Before we could explore the area around where we were staying with the Rotheras, we had some serious shopping to do, so a trip into town, to the *dukha* or shops, was planned. Before leaving England we had bought some twenty rolls of Agfa 35 mm colour slide film and unanimously decided to keep to the same format for uniformity. We were worried because we had already used half of our film supply just on the journey and one trip into the game park. Ian, being the 'professional' photographer, was concerned that the colour temperature could change from different batches of film. The main

Agfa supplier in Nairobi assured us, that in their film we, or any audience, would never notice any small discrepancy in the change of colour or 'colour temperature' between pictures. We emerged from the Agfa place very happy, with a special deal on thirty more films to add to the twenty rolls we already had.

Next stop, at Ian's insistence, was a camera shop recommended by the chap at the Agfa store. Having chosen a telephoto 135 mm Lieca lens, Ian was determined to try some photos to make sure that the lens was up to the mark. It was an expensive lens although cheaper than from home, and the shop owner gave Ian a receipt for about two thirds of the actual price paid in order to reduce the amount of import duty he would have to pay at Dover on our return to England. It would have been a long way to take it back under warranty! So with some pictures exposed, the test film was taken to be developed at the Agfa store where we were assured that it would be ready the next day. A welcome and hearty lunch was then consumed at Nairobi's second outstanding establishment the Norfolk Hotel. We certainly ate well whilst we were in Kenya!

I had been very impressed with the safari boots, which I had earlier bought at Frank's suggestion, and which some of the other local younger men wore. A kind of bush uniform, they were made of thick suede leather, which gave some ankle support and protection from insects and thorns. Frank reckoned that they helped against snakebites. Whereas I thought that knee length boots were more appropriate, I appreciated that they were too bulky and hot to wear continually and too expensive to buy anyway. Frank did like winding us all up though from time to time; part of his character, but he did seem to enjoy having us all with him on this vacation. I did find the boots most comfortable and hard wearing and actually bought two spare pairs to take back to the UK.

We found a local wholesale distributor who willingly gave us a good deal on a carton of Sportsman cigarettes made from homegrown Kenyan tobacco and a case of locally brewed Tuskers lager-type continental beer to wash down the incessant dust. I found it interesting that the Indian community, whose ancestors had originally been brought to East Africa from India to build the railway from the coast to lake Victoria, now seemed to run the shops and small businesses throughout the region.

One store, which grabbed our attention though, was a tool shop. We had never seen anything like this before as it catered for the whole of East Africa's farming, transport and mechanical engineering requirements. The range of spanners and sockets was phenomenal from very small BA sizes to 3 inch AF and with every conceivable tool ever required available from stock, a most remarkable place.

We also decided to call in to see the official agent for the English Electric Co. Ltd. who had an office in town. We found him in, a rare occasion, as he covered the whole of the Uganda, Kenya and Tanganyika countries. We spent an interesting hour filling him in with detail of what was going on with the company in the UK and also he gave us info on what to do and where to go! It was then of course that we really appreciated the vast range of products and exports that our workforce produced. Whilst the factories at Stafford mainly concentrated on high voltage power generation and transmission control equipment, the sister companies throughout England produced a range of products as diverse as trains to planes and marine engines to domestic and household electrical goods. The company was also involved with the early design and manufacture of computer systems. At that time, it seemed inconceivable that most of that manufacturing expertise and capacity would be virtually gone within forty years, with the remnants of the Stafford plant now owned by a French conglomerate.

Frank's parents knew the owners of a hotel establishment at Thika near a spectacular array of waterfalls known as Fourteen Falls, which was the base from which many of the early Tarzan films were shot. Good use was made of that area particularly for the dramatic water and falls scenes of the films. As we climbed down a steep path at the side of the cascade, we almost expected to see Johnny Weissmuller to come swinging through the canopy of trees surrounding the river. The hotel had often provided a civilised headquarters for the film company's entourage and we were told that many famous people had stayed there.

Whilst only a few miles away from the Rotheras, the hotel also boasted a swimming pool and we had been invited to pop in for a swim any time we wanted. (Well nearer thirty miles in reality but considered local and this just puts into perspective the vast distances it was necessary to travel if we wanted to see the country). So one lovely sunny afternoon, soon after our arrival in Kenya, we found ourselves standing at the end of the 50 yards pool, which was a very good length for a hotel pool. With our pale skin, we obviously looked like the four new blokes just out from the dank UK, for as yet we had hardly got our knees brown.

Now I used to do a lot of swimming back in my school days, so in order to impress the local talent, I suddenly decided to dive into the pool with a racing start and swim to the far end at a quick pace. I had thought originally to do two lengths as a warm up, but half way down the first length my arms and legs felt like lead and I was fighting for breath. Not wanting the talent or my friends to think I was a wimp, I pushed on to the end of the pool absolutely exhausted and vowing to get fit again and give up smoking. As I sat on the side nonchalantly taking in the view and trying to recover, Frank appeared with remarks like "That'll teach you" and "You aren't at home now, we are at 5500 ft, you must get acclimatised". Yes, I just did not realise that the relative lack of oxygen at that height was such a factor. A period of acclimatisation was certainly needed. Being short sighted and not wearing my glasses for the swim, I had not realised that the group of young ladies giggling at the side, were in fact younger than I had thought. I needn't have bothered showing off my swimming ability!

We were invited to tea at the farm near to the bungalow where we stayed, and whilst being informed that afternoon tea would be at 4 o'clock precisely, we could arrive earlier and be shown around the farm. The farmer, Jack Stevens, was one of the old school of colonial gentlemen whose grandfather had been one of the early pioneer settlers, forming the landscape into a homestead and farm, soon after the railway was built. His balding and thinning grey hair with his weather-beaten face emphasised the fact that he had lived all his life in this environment, but the sparkle in his eye hinted that we would have an interesting afternoon. The farm was a complete mixture of dairy and arable, with some coffee and tea plantation too. This was because the farm lay across the soil and altitude suitable for both types of crop. The coffee was grown up to a certain altitude and then the tea plantation reached the higher ground. Having come from a rural background myself, I was very interested to see that the dairy and other farm activities were similar to those of England.

Jack Stevens was nearing the completion of a big project of building a dam, plus access road so that the water could be used for an hydroelectric power supply as well as for irrigation purposes when necessary, or if the rains were late. Jack asked his farm manager, a pleasant Indian man in his thirties, to drive us down to the dam and show us his project, whilst he did the important job of organising tea. After alighting from the Land Rover near the earthworks of the dam, the others wandered down on to the dam itself, whereas I climbed up a grassy bank for a picture view of the landscape of undulating hills reaching into the distance. I then found it was necessary for me to change the film in my camera, (a problem which I seem to have at inappropriate times even today!)

Whilst I was doing this, I was surprised, but thankfully not alarmed, by the silent approach of an elderly native gentleman who came and sat down beside me. He wore the seemingly traditional British kaki battle dress top with the native skirt or kikois but no footwear or headwear. He placed his spear and bow with a quiver of arrows down on the grass beside him. Whilst we each smoked a Sportsman cigarette, he told me how the landscape had changed over the years and about his involvement with the farm for most of his life. He was intensely proud of this land and by his description of the bird and wildlife still around, he was sincerely concerned about conservation. I found the experience very humbling; here was I talking to an elderly native in his country, for the conversation was all in my language. For a private enterprise, the dam and resulting lake were quite large. Whilst the pump house and turbine building had been completed the actual installation of the machinery and corresponding electrical wiring and power cables still had to be finished. There was more than a hint of suggestion that we four visitors should get on with it!

The farmhouse was the original, as built in the early nineteen hundreds, but had been extensively modified and extended to cope with the growing family community of the estate. Rather like some of the large farmhouses and halls of Britain. The immaculately dressed houseboy showed us into the drawing room, where we were greeted enthusiastically by the old farmer himself who asked us,

"What tea would you prefer?" We were all a bit flummoxed as we thought that Kenyan tea would be like the standard Typhoo or Brook

Bond teas from our home. Consequently we were escorted to the parlour and proudly shown the largest selection of teas I had ever seen. Probably on a par with those at Brook Bond themselves. He even had samples of teas from over the years, all labelled and preserved in airtight tins. Jack enthused about them like the maître seigneur from a vineyard, telling us about the good years and the not so good ones and which blends were created for special occasions over the years.

To a lesser extent the coffee crop was sorted into blends and years as well but it was the tea that held the fascination for this remarkable old colonialist. It was nice to be taken back in time, for the setting was that of a late Victorian or Edwardian afternoon tea party with cucumber sandwiches and muffins accompanying the chosen teas, all served up by the impeccably mannered houseboy, on delicate china from the Staffordshire Potteries. We did not disgrace ourselves and remembered our table manners too, as we listened to Mozart being played on an old phonograph and enjoyed the lively conversation. It was only our dress that portrayed the time of the sixties instead of that of half a century earlier.

Our travels also took us to a large and traditional coffee plantation. In fact 'Bano Farm Estates of Kiambu' was one of the oldest and best plantations in Kenya. Dave Wells, the son of the owners and a friend of Frank, took us on an interesting and detailed tour of the workings of the plantation, from the planting and care of the coffee bushes to the picking, drying and grading of the beans. There was, as in all things, a lot more to coffee farming than we had imagined. We were told that some smaller plantations were up for sale, usually because the European owners had decided to return to their roots. A changing political climate also encouraged others to move down to South Africa, nevertheless the opportunity was there for enterprising persons to get into that lucrative business. We were strongly encouraged to consider the purchase of a farm at a very realistic price. It was certainly food for thought. The idea appealed to each one in a different way, but the different life style and distance from our families back in England brought us all back down to earth. Who knows, perhaps it would not be just another dream.

Paradise! That was the impression I had when I looked out from the lounge of the old plantation house. The room was quite dark but tastefully filled with antique furniture and ornaments collected over many years. The open double French Windows led into a loggia with exotic plants and shrubs strategically placed about. Trees, branches and vines spread from both side walls up and over the roof, and extended outside where the bright sunshine caused the foliage to almost sparkle. This explained why it had seemed quite dark inside the house. As I stepped through the open doors into that most unusual setting, the muted noisy chatter became louder and apparent as bird song, but a bird song I had never heard before. The movement and brilliant colours of many species of little birds coupled with that natural chorus was absolutely magical, a setting normally only portrayed in the movies.

We walked between the supporting columns of the loggia on to the patio, and took our seats at a giant rustic hardwood table still sheltered from the heat of the early afternoon sun by the trees and foliage. The birds seemed everywhere, and it was a little while before any of us realised that we were in fact sitting in a gigantic aviary cunningly constructed to keep certain birds in, yet allow other wild birds access, to also enjoy the feeding pots scattered amongst the branches or on the floor.

An African Grey parrot eyed us with interest as it wandered around its perches sticking out of a post at eye level near to the doorway. This was complimented by a green and yellow parrot on a similar perch on the other side of the door. They looked like two sentries guarding the exquisite aviary and I had the impression that they had been there since the house had been built! As I looked out on to a perfect lawn, the peacocks paraded their magnificent tail plumes as if on cue to the conductor of the orchestra. However I was drawn to the movement of other ferret-type creatures playing near to a low 2 ft wire mesh fence on the edge of the lawn. These were mongoose and like the peacocks, played a useful purpose in this beautiful establishment. They were an early warning and protection against uninvited intruders. The mongoose gave confidence to the adults to allow children to play on the lawns, as they would keep snakes away whilst the peacocks' shrieking call would alert everybody of any other danger. It was a fantastic idea. We were all so over-whelmed by the theatrical occasion that we never noticed the houseboys bring refreshments out on to the patio for our benefit.

Chapter 8

Tree Tops

There were many highlights of our adventures out in Kenya, and many memories, which would be related by us over the years to follow. One of these highlights was to visit the special reserve of the 'Aberdare National Park', the home of Tree Tops, for that famous game viewing lodge, which had royal connections, was built literally up in the trees. We were grateful to Frank's parents who had kindly treated us to a nights stay at this historic enterprise. First however, the six of us, in two cars the Beetle and the 1500, had to make the journey north. So we headed out on the Thika road, then via Fort Hall to Nyeri in the foothills of the Aberdare Mountains. We were now only about 25 miles from the equator but at nearly 6500 ft above sea level.

The normal routine for visiting Tree Tops was to meet for lunch at the Outspan Hotel situated on the edge of the game park. Trips into the park could be arranged from there in a Land Rover with a guide, quite necessary for not getting lost in that unforgiving territory. We were all greatly amused by the sight of a very docile zebra all saddled up to give rides to children. Fortunately we were all too old for such an adventure, so we ventured into the hotel restaurant encouraged by the appetising odours for what promised to be a tasty lunch. We were all famished and were not in the least disappointed. Later as we climbed into the hotel's minibus, we wondered if we should have eaten a little less, for we did not know how far or how rough the dirt track up to Tree Tops itself would be!

I peered out from the protection of the stockade to the next one some 50 yards away. The white hunter at my side held the heavy duty rifle, a true elephant gun at the ready. No one spoke, but on his signal, the six of us stealthily walked to the next point of safety, the next stockade. We could now see Tree Tops clearly in the distance as we emerged from some bushes. A grey wooden building perched in a giant *mgumu* tree and supported by pylons driven into the solid earth. It looked a bit top heavy but I thought that on reflection that most tree houses did too. But this was a big one. On reaching the next and last stockade before the final push to the safety of the building itself, I glanced back and saw another party progressing as equally cautious as ourselves with another hunter or guard following behind.

We were assured that no hostile animals were very close. Nevertheless precautions were necessary, for only a couple of weeks previously, a small group had been entrapped in a stockade while an elephant, looking for a young one, was coaxed away. The experience of having to walk through the bush dramatised the scenario and accentuated the spectacular sighting of this famous game lodge. We climbed the wooden steps up into the lodge itself and settled ourselves in, while our luggage was brought up from the Outspan Hotel by porters and deposited into our small bunk bedded rooms. It was not long before all the guests were assembled on to the flat roof terrace of the lodge looking expectantly for wildlife.

At the one end of the roof terrace was a bronze plaque mounted on a wooden frame. The inscription described the connection of Tree Tops with the British royal family and explained the saying of 'The girl who became queen in a tree'.

**IN THIS MGUMU TREE
HER ROYAL HIGHNESS THE PRINCESS ELIZABETH
AND
HIS ROYAL HIGHNESS THE DUKE OF EDINBURGH
SPENT THE NIGHT OF FEBRUARY 5TH 1952
WHILE HERE PRINCESS ELIZABETH
SUCCEEDED TO THE THRONE
THROUGH THE DEATH OF HER FATHER
KING GEORGE THE SIXTH**

The waterhole was only some thirty yards away and obviously varied in size depending on the amount of rainfall. There was however, a second allure for some of the animals, apart from a drinking place. Natural salt deposits gave this venue the importance of being a giant salt lick too. This attracted elephant and rhino along with many varieties of buck and so naturally enough their predators as well. I was excited to see a small group of elephants, with a young one who seemed determined to get himself into trouble. The normally fairly dark grey colour of the elephant skins were covered in the traditional red dust and mud so prevalent out in Kenya, and this gave the animals a reddish tinge, the original pink elephant. The youngster kept trying to get into the pool but the adults stopped it after allowing it to drink of course. Whilst the pool was too small to house crocodile or hippopotamus, perhaps the adults thought it was too deep for the young elephant. Whatever the reason they would not let it venture far into the water.

Warthogs, a distant cousin to the domesticated pigs normally found on farms, although more closely related to wild boar, seemed to be a very brave but aggressive animal. A couple of them appeared, but were not put off from drinking by the antics of the elephants, who certainly did not like these creatures anywhere near their baby! Although not particularly very big, these quite ugly omnivores, with the wart-like lumps on their faces, used the vicious looking tusks to root in the ground for anything edible. These tusks I was certain, were very useful weapons if the case arose, but the hogs I am sure, seemed to delight in provoking the elephants into chasing them around the pool. A lone large water buffalo appeared to quench its thirst and gave the appearance of co-existence with the elephant. I was surprised how big the buffalo actually was and was amused that the hogs now had a new neighbour to exasperate. We all took plenty of photographs, but I was envious of Ian using his new telephoto lens. This was certainly one situation that needed an appropriate lens in order to get close to the action. Perhaps one day I would find a long lens for my camera.

Afternoon tea seemed to be a tradition of colonial society out in Kenya. At the due time, the waiters dressed in their smart uniforms, brought out the food and drinks for the guests staying at the lodge. However, we were very quickly joined at the party by a troop of baboons, whose speed across the ground from the trees at the far side of the pool, and whose agility at climbing up to the terrace, had to be seen to be believed. Hardly had the trays been placed on the tables than the monkeys were amongst every one and they didn't bother to politely queue either. Whilst not having much to eat ourselves, we did have the opportunity of taking some close up photos, if we could be quick enough. The whole tea party, like the walk up to the lodge itself added to the experience of our visit and we were absolutely delighted that the baboons sat around on the terrace guardrails, posing like true professionals for photographs. As the great orange orb sank into the earth, throwing the lengthening shadows across the savannah scrub, the darkness leapt out as if from nowhere to take over from that glorious day. The sounds of the wild had now changed the ambience, so we were pleased to be in the safety of the lodge. We shivered, and not just from the cold, as we made our way down to the dining room. We were still hoping to see more wild life as the evening progressed.

The restaurant was quite compact, a necessity of the building being perched up a tree, so the extended dining room table had long bench type, but none the less comfortable seating, on either side. It meant that when people were seated, there was no space for the waiters to serve in the normal manner. This problem was ingeniously overcome by a railway line traversing the length of the table with the 'flat bed rolling stock', carrying all the important components for a good meal, running up and down the table at the beck and call of the twenty or so impatient diners. As the evening progressed the speed of the train also progressed to the point of really testing the bumpers at either end of the line!

After the main course, it was suggested that someone ought to have a look to see if any more game had arrived at the watering hole under cover of darkness. The area across to the pool and a little beyond, had been floodlit to enable guests to watch any animals which came to drink, for they were quite used to that particular area of the park being illuminated, and it didn't seem to bother them at all.

I, being seated at the end of the table, volunteered to investigate whether anything interesting was happening outside, so I quietly stepped out on to the balcony adjacent to the dining room to survey the scene by the waterhole. We had seen many things so far on our travels, but the feelings I had when I looked out on to the lighted area surrounded by pitch black were almost overwhelming. Standing just a few feet below me was a rhinoceros. He was a very big lad indeed, so much bigger than the rhino I had previously seen at Chester zoo. The sound of a gasp in my breathing caused him to look straight at me, for although they have relatively poor eyesight, rhino have very acute hearing. I was the creature in the cage now being observed by one of the inhabitants of this fascinating land. I reported back to the dining room and everyone made a beeline for the balconies. The rhino nonchalantly wandered over to drink from the pool, probably to get away from the sounds of twenty or so people trying to move quietly to comfortable seating in the viewing platforms. I shall never forget my first glimpse of that magnificent animal just a few feet from me.

Yes, the captivating sounds of the bush at night had certainly set the ambiance of the whole place for the next few hours, as the nocturnal creatures ventured forth. The grunts and snorts of the warthogs still intimidating the buffalo or trying to separate the young elephant from its family. The distant cackle of hyena laughing at some poor trapped or injured animal trying to escape. The excited chatter of a troop of baboons warning of the prowling of a big cat, probably a lion, in search of another kill. The commotion of a small flock of unknown birds disturbed from their roost by some unknown predator on the lookout for an easy meal. Thousands of tree frogs tuned in to add their chorus to the nocturne of the evening. The banging and crashing of a big elephant in the wooded copse, who having finally lost his patience with the warthogs, decided to drive every one away from his patch.

The trumpeting and exasperations of the bad tempered elephant, pushing and shoving between the support piling of the lodge in his quest to be rid of the buffalo, did cause us all some concern. Would those heavy-duty posts stand up to a fight between these two very large animals? We all certainly very much hoped so, as we did not want to be caught up in that tussle. The large buffalo, however, did not want to be moved, so the antics of that skirmish continued throughout the night. It was later, on reflecting about that night spent out in the bush, that I realised that many of the so-called nocturnal animals were active during the day as well and vice versa. Perhaps that was why one saw so few animals during the main part of the day, they were all trying to catch up on some sleep!

After an early start with tea and biscuits, we were all ushered back to the Outspan Hotel for a hearty breakfast and a debriefing of our experiences at the famous Tree Tops game lodge. The six of us were now ready to continue our trip northwards and over the Equator to Thomson's Falls. We skirted east of the Aberdare Mountains and up the large, mainly flat valley, before crossing the Equator just west of Mount Kenya. The sight of the majestic Mount Kenya rising up from the plain to over 17000 ft was most impressive, and whilst often covered in cloud, we were fortunate to glimpse the summit, covered in snow, peeping through the light patchy cloud covering that day.

Elephant grass dominated the area around the mountain, which was of course the home to some elephant herds as well. We had heard horror stories of people being trapped on the narrow paths through the very tall almost bamboo type of vegetation with the razor sharp grasses, which could cut a human to pieces. If one met an elephant there was just nowhere to escape to. The African elephant towers over its Indian cousin with a large bull being about twice the size of the semi-domesticated Indian elephant, so caution was the better part of valour and we kept away from the elephant grass which incidentally concealed snakes and other creatures too. I remember, from a magazine, a classic picture of some African Elephants, a sunset and the snow-capped Mount Kenya in the background. I never thought at that time, I would one day actually be driving through the savannah close to that mountain. It was so easy to forget that the whole scenario was actually on the Equator!

As the endless road crossed the point of 0 deg. Latitude, the sign showing that we were actually on the Equator intrigued us. I didn't really think that there would be a line or band circumnavigating the Earth, but naively expected more than a yellow board picturing a black map of Africa and a red line depicting the Equator. In reality though we were on a remote track at above 7700 ft, in the back of beyond in the African bush, and *this* was the main road to the North. I suppose that we were fortunate that there was actually a sign to tell people that the Equator crossed the road at that point. We laughed and recounted the scientific experiment, the Coriolis effect, to tell where the Equator actually was. The water down the plughole hypothesis, where the water drains out, with a clockwise spout in the northern hemisphere *but* an anticlockwise in the southern hemisphere. I had actually seen a film to show this, with a small stick floating on the bowl turning to the right or the left as appropriate, and it only needed a few yards from the equatorial line to instigate the direction of flow from the bowl. Remarkably the stick stayed still and the water flowed straight down at the Equator. This phenomenon is said to be caused by the rotation of the Earth on its axis.

The small township of Thomson's Falls at 7740 ft, lay virtually on the Equator at the confluence of two tributaries and a spectacular waterfall feeding the river, which was making its way to the desolate plains of the north and east. This river initially passed through the highland forests, then through very dense scrub punctuated by areas of swampland. These were nurtured by the countless streams and rivulets, constantly fed by the mountain range behind us and of course by Mount Kenya which dominated the plateau to our right. I found the maps of this area most intriguing. Produced by the British Ordnance Survey organisation, the detail shown of that wild and barren landscape read just like a book, (to me anyway). One of the situations I could only surmise was how does a river, which flows all year round, disappear into brush and swamp and only reappear during the rainy season? The maps also gave guidance on the state of the roads, or rather very rough tracks with comments such as *'motorable'*, *'dry weather only'*, *'motorable with difficulty'* etc. The terrain itself was certainly very inhospitable, but was not the only danger, for that place was home to many, many animals of all shapes and sizes, which were very dangerous too.

On the road above the river stood a lone hostelry, a remarkably unique trading post, café bar and pub combined, for this was the first roadside restaurant we three foreigners had seen out in Kenya. Outside was parked one of the conspicuous zebra mini buses along with a couple of cars. Quite a busy place I thought. Certainly a welcoming oasis for dusty and weary travellers to take refreshments, as we had travelled well over one hundred miles, since leaving Nairobi, with only a very few of those miles on tarmac. Inside the relative cool of the café bar were gathered a few of the tourists washing the red dust from out of their throats with a sample of the local Tusker beer. Apart from the guests at the reserve the previous evening, they were the first tourists we had seen close up, comprising mainly of Germans and Americans. We seemed to be the only British *'tourists'*, for Kenya at that time was not a normal holiday destination. They were going to the Samburu game lodge and seemed surprised that we Englanders had actually visited Tree Tops. I thought this just showed the remoteness of the different game parks scattered over the plains of Africa.

As young electrical engineers, we were invited to look around the old 60 KVA power-station driven by the river, a useful source of hydroelectric power, and were intrigued by and interested to see that much of the equipment used had been made in England by 'our' English Electric Co. We then took lunch at Barry's Hotel, which was where David and Edna Rothera were managers in the early 1950s. On leaving Thomson's Falls, the two cars headed southwards again, back over the Equator and down the west side of the Aberdare Mountains before descending the escarpment into the Great African Rift Valley to Naivasha with its famous flamingo lake. It was whilst having tea there that Bunny realised that he had somehow lost his watch, probably at the waterfalls which we had previously visited. Frank reckoned that it was more likely that some monkey from Tree Tops was wearing it!

We had joined one of the few good tarmac roads of the region, built by Italian prisoners of war during the later part of World War 11, to provide good access from Nairobi to Kampala in Uganda and to supplement the Railway built half a century earlier. Part way up the steep escarpment out of the Rift Valley stands a small church also built by the prisoners and I thought about the remoteness of this, as no other buildings were seen for miles until we turned off to Limuru and across White Highland country to 'Residence Rothera'. During the evening we all chatted enthusiastically about the most enjoyable couple of days we had spent exploring this amazing land with its breathtaking scenery and remarkable wildlife. That night I shuddered as I dreamt of what it may have been like to camp out under canvas in that wild and dangerous country.

Chapter 9

Motor Sport

As we explored the area around the White Highlands, we were all fascinated with the endless number of dirt roads available for us to negotiate, and we felt that it would have been a real bonus to be in Kenya for the Safari Rally, which was at that time traditionally held over the Easter week. Inaugurated in 1952 for the coronation of Queen Elizabeth II, the Safari Rally was considered by most competitors and observers alike, to be the longest and toughest motor rally in the world. Swede Eric Carlson and his British wife Pat Moss, driving Saab 96s, both led the 1962 event at different times. Pat succumbed to an impala jumping out and severely damaging the front of the car on the last day with consequent loss of time and the chance of a win.

It took 22 years before a works European driver, Timo Makinen in the Ford Escort, was able to break the stranglehold of the local drivers on this prestigious event. The roads were so tough that local knowledge was deemed absolutely necessary to cope with the changeable conditions as the rally tore through the dust, mud and water of an ever-changing landscape; for in those days the route also included Uganda and Tanganyika as well as Kenya. Oh, to have been able to compete, but we had to make do with make believe. We did though get some great photos of the black Beetle enveloped in clouds of thick red African dust.

Volkswagen agents and importers the Cooper Motor Corporation had a large garage complex in Nairobi catering for the expansive East African region. There was a saying that 'two makes of cars were popular out there. Ford because one could get spare parts and VW because one didn't need any'. Nevertheless there were also quite a few Peugeot vehicles and of course the British Land Rover, which was in its element on the very types of terrain that it was made for. However in reality, all vehicles need maintenance and so, particularly as young engineers and motor enthusiasts, we were very pleased to be invited by the service manager to look around the extensive Volkswagen workshops.

At that time all VW vehicles, cars such as Beetles and 1500s together with the Combi variants of minibuses, vans and pickup trucks, had the same wheel base; this enabled the servicing to be carried out on an almost 'production line' type of arrangement. Because of the comparative lack of good tarmac roads in East Africa at that time, even the average vehicle had to endure in one year, what would be a lifetimes abuse in England. The rough surface with the endless potholes made the suspension work very hard indeed, and when the terrain wasn't dusty then the red sticky mud filled up every nook and cranny, adding considerable weight to the vehicle.

However it was the incessant dust, which caused most problems to the engine; where filters and oil needed to be changed often. So servicing on a regular basis was indeed a necessity, particularly as most people lived miles from 'civilization'. Each vehicle had a general wash off before being raised off the ground at the front, to enable the operative to thoroughly steam clean the underneath and the engine compartment; the position of which varied with each model. The vehicle was then pushed on to a trolley, which then joined the service line. Wheels off, brakes stripped, shock absorbers and suspension arms checked and of course the steering system.

The engine was almost stripped to clean out the abrasive dust, whilst the ignition components and carburettors were stripped and cleaned too, before being fitted with any necessary new parts. In fact, each service was a major one, but we were told it was the only way to keep a vehicle running in that country. We were most impressed by all of this and pleased to be told that our faithful Beetle had been through this same rigour prior to our arrival. They must have guessed as to how many miles and the kind of terrain we intended to explore.

Ironically, the only 'breakdown' we had with the Beetle was when we, or rather Frank as he was driving, ran out of petrol. Now those early VWs. did not have a petrol gauge, just a reserve petrol tap like most motorcycles of that era, and so Franks estimation that we had enough juice to get us back to town caused us to walk a mile or so to the Agip petrol station on the edge of Nairobi. We later felt grateful that we only had to walk that far, particularly as garages were pretty scarce when out of town. It was a lesson for us to make sure that we were full up, before every trip of exploration into the wild and desolate country surrounding the relative civilisation of Nairobi and its environs.

Dave Wells had invited us to spend an evening with the 'East African Motor Club'. We immediately felt at home as the whole of the conversations were about cars, motor sport and forth-coming events. Whilst we had regularly been to the meetings of our home motor club in England, the 'Potteries and Newcastle Motor Club', we had not been able to compete very much during the summer of 1966 because of the costs and work to be done for our Kenya trip. So the whole evening stimulated and nurtured us like a tonic to our motor sport deficient minds. When they asked us to help out at a national race meeting being held the following weekend up at their racetrack at Nakuru, we certainly did not take much persuasion, we were delighted to go. So a few days later, Bunny and Ian, with Dave in his Fiat 850 and myself with Frank in the VW, set out to Nakuru, 100 miles north west of Nairobi and about 20 miles south of the Equator.

Nakuru at above 6000 ft is sited in the Rift Valley, nestled between the Menengai Crater and the picturesque lake of the same name. It lies also on the crossroads of both the main road and rail links of Nairobi and Uganda to the west. The old giant volcano of Menengai has an impressive shallow calderas, (a very large crater) of 7 miles across, caused by the collapsing of the mountain cone into the void left by the rock and magna during eruption.

Later we visited another volcano with a very different type of crater. However it was this small lake at Nakuru, only about 4 miles by 6 miles, which claimed our attention. It was said that it was possible to see more that two million flame-pink flamingos paddling about in the soda-saturated water in search of shrimps and other crustaceans along with the blue-green algae formed by the unique geographical location of the lake. At nearly 6000 ft, being close to the equator with sunlight all year round to grow the algae and the closeness of the volcanic action supplying its cocktail of soda chemicals to sustain the food chain, the lake was able to support this incredible flock of flamingos. There were two of the world's six species present, the greater flamingo reaching nearly 6 ft, which will eat crustaceans and algae and its cousin the lesser flamingo only about half the size, which mainly eats algae. The sight and sounds of this vast colony taking to the deep blue skies, as if one gigantic creature, is why Lake Nakuru is called the greatest bird spectacle in the world.

Our main reason for being at Nakuru that particular weekend was of course because of the motor races being held at the club's track near to the township. Although this was a national event there were a few visiting drivers from Uganda, as it was not many more miles to the border. Big mileages never seemed to bother people living out in East Africa though, as it was always necessary to travel large distances, often on difficult roads, if one wanted to go anywhere. The paddock located in the centre of the circuit was quite full by the time we arrived, and was a frenzy of activity as drivers, riders and mechanics scurried around the biggest assortment of racing machinery that I had ever seen at any race meeting before. There was a good turnout of saloon and modified production cars with a few enterprising specials complementing a handful of single seater racecars too.

Still the big difference between British and African motor sport was the inclusion of motorcycles, something I had never seen before, although I had heard from my father about combined meetings held in England during the 1930s. So we were to witness racing for two, three and four wheeled vehicles on a good tarmac surfaced track with interesting corners and slightly undulating terrain. I purposely say three wheels, as these were motorbike and sidecar, otherwise known as a motorcycle combination or in racing jargon an outfit, which always attracted attention from their charismatic characters when racing. Among the sidecar fraternity was a lone Morgan three-wheeler car. Two wheels, either side of the exposed V twin J.A.P motorcycle engine, at the front and one at the rear, made this a truly unusual sporting vehicle, which was traditionally allowed to compete with the motorcycle combinations, but was sadly now outclassed in speed and road holding. Many individuals however, just like to compete and were happy to drive whatever they could; the more interesting the better. This was club motor sport at its very best, as all competitors were very enthusiastic amateurs who had brought their families with them to act in the various roles necessary for a successful race team! Surveying the colourful spectacle of tents, trailers and vans littering the paddock, we looked forward with anticipation to an exciting event.

Being from a motorcycle background I was particularly interested in two Sikh Indian brothers with a well designed and carefully prepared racing motorcycle outfit. This three-wheeled contraption certainly looked the part and sounded terrific with its big Triumph Speed-Twin engine in full flight. These two brothers were good engineers and did all their own work, and then raced the outfit as well as solo machines too. I laughed to myself when off came the turbans and on went the helmets as they went out for their turn to practice and set up the bikes for the conditions. In the UK the motorcycle helmet law had been introduced amid the controversy of compulsion, with some riders protesting about having to wear a safety helmet. Some of these protesters were Sikhs complaining on religious grounds that they could not remove their turban. I wished that they could have seen these two brothers in action on the racetrack and then in the paddock with turbans neatly replaced!

Practice was a fairly standard affair, with most competitors wanting to make sure that their pride and joy would survive to race the next day. A few spins and an occasional overshoot at the top hairpin was all that caused any real excitement. But just to be there, soaking in the atmosphere and savouring the smell of 'Castrol R', the special racing oil used predominately in motorcycle engines, was all that we wanted. We all certainly enjoyed simply being in attendance. Our main forte was rallying, which was a relatively lonely activity, particularly in the days of long distance events, so it was a welcome contrast to be part of that social and gregarious group assembled in the middle of Africa that weekend. A good meal at the local hotel at Nakuru and a couple of beers around the campfire back at the racetrack, whilst listening to experiences and horror stories from the Safari Rally, all added to the enjoyment of the day.

Sleeping arrangements were nonetheless a bit basic. What should we expect though for we could have stayed at the hotel and missed half the fun. We were told that we could camp out in the pavilion adjacent to the grandstand by the start and finish line of the racetrack. We found three camp beds and a hammock. Dave grabbed the hammock as he had slept in one before, whilst Bunny, Ian and I had a camp bed. Frank in his normal tradition under that situation just slept on the grass by the door, for he would sleep anywhere. Ian reckoned that Frank could sleep on a clothesline, whilst I have known him to actually sleep in a car traversing a forest track at high speed, during a special stage on an international car rally, but that is another story.

The explosive sound of a racing engine bursting into life at some ridiculous early hour of the morning awakened us, even though daylight had already arrived. A reveille perhaps to call the competitors to their post as racing was due to start at 10 am, and there was as always, a lot of last minute preparations to do. A clear blue sky greeted us as we came out of the pavilion all bleary eyed and made our way again to the latrines tucked away and hopefully down wind from the main camp in the paddock. We met Frank, who was wide-awake and had inevitably slept better than the rest of us, drinking some coffee that he had scrounged from the organisers. We could have some too! Oh, the price? He had volunteered us to help with the official time keeping during the racing.

We had not got long before we would be needed to learn what to do. As we traipsed across to the ablutions, Frank warned us with his infectious laugh to be on the lookout for creatures. Now I had been used to 'facilities' at race meetings, particularly at temporary venues on some friendly farmers land back home in Shropshire, as my dad was always involved with motor sport events of one sort or another.

We approached the two canvassed structures with our need overcoming the pong permeating from the latrines. A hand painted sign differentiated between ladies and gents so we entered the latter. The canvas walled area held up by poles, housed a couple of cubicles with a canvas flap door, containing a galvanised bucket with a basic wooden toilet seat perched on top. The whole space was open to the sky. Continuing through a rear doorway we found the urinal, a trench along the back canvas wall running into a hole used as a soak away. This was also just open to the bush and we laughed at the thought of no privacy for us. I wondered if any watching animals would have been confused, by so many males marking the same patch with their scent.

The odour of Jays fluid told of some attempt to provide some sanitation, although the heat of the day would exasperate any attempt to quench the smell, the insects were still the biggest problem to control. It was fortunate that the facility was only being used for one day! "Did we find any creatures"? Frank asked on our return. "Only insects" we replied. "No black widows then?" Frank added with another infectious laugh. I inferred that they were in Australia, but he laughed even more and told us that Africa had its own. Another Frank joke I thought as he continued to wind us up, nevertheless we were always very cautious when we ventured back into the latrines.

Back down by the pavilion we found some water in a bucket which was suitable for basic ablutions and the luxury of a battery electric razor with the use of a car's wing mirror, as per our journey through Europe, meant that at least we could freshen up a bit. So now looking and feeling a little more respectable, the five of us gathered in the timekeepers' section of the grandstand awaiting our briefing. The job in hand was to record the actual lap time and total time of each competitor during the race. Each timekeeper was allocated a limited number of cars etc to record for each race. This was done by the use of three stopwatches, two used for lap times and the third for total race time. A moveable bar across the top of the board on which the clocks were mounted enabled the timekeeper to start and stop two watches simultaneously at the exact moment when a competitor crossed the start/finish line of the racetrack immediately below us.

All that we had to do then was to record the time of that lap and reset the watch to be restarted at the appropriate instance, then to also record the race time on the same official sheet. Once we got into the system we found it quite easy, so we could watch the racing, although always being aware of the progress of our own racers. From the relative luxury of the timekeepers' section in the grandstand, we had excellent vision of nearly the entire racetrack, which enhanced our enjoyment of the day.

When the start flag was dropped, the roar of the engines as the pack rocketed away from the grid, coupled with the squeal of tyres desperately trying to find some grip on the hot tarmac, whilst the contestants attempted to negotiate the first right hand corner, certainly emphasised the excitement of true amateur motor sport at its best. The two Indian brothers were in a league of their own in the sidecar races and one won a solo race as well. The Lotus Cortina of Peter Hughes and Vic Preston, of Safari Rally fame, was extremely quick and well driven, so as expected, annihilated the opposition. There were a few shunts when over enthusiastic drivers tried to overtake in an impossible situation on the inside of a corner, or thought that they had got better brakes than they had. A Mini Cooper rolled after overcorrecting a big slide, probably practicing the rally drivers' technique of 'left foot braking', easier said than done on tarmac! A couple of the motorcycle riders slid off their bikes whilst trying to out-brake each other into a tight left-hander. Fortunately from these incidents no one was hurt, other than a few bruises and some dents to machinery and pride.

During a break in the proceedings for a spot of lunch, which none of us had thought to bring, we realized how hot it was getting, particularly out in the bush, for we were very lucky to be in the shade of the grandstand. Certainly Bunny, Ian and myself were not used to the tropical sun, and I am sure would have been burnt up had we been out on the racetrack marshalling. As I looked about I realized that there were no shadows! The awesome sun was at its zenith, directly overhead, and appeared to have bleached the colour out of the sky with just brilliant light all above and heat haze in the distance. We hunted about for some refreshments, when Bunny reminded us that we had not had a real breakfast, and we were thankful to the families of some officials for taking pity on us poor starving lads. Ian made a mental note, as catering manager; to make sure we had plenty of food and drink with us on our future exploits.

The afternoons racing continued with the same enthusiasm as before, with most competitors now trying even harder to better their position in the point's league. There was no let-up in the activities, as the races followed each other in quick succession. The organisation was very slick. It needed to be as the weather was at last changing. The storm clouds gathered on the horizon, threatened to dampen the ardour of the race meeting. Fortunately it was only the last saloon car race that succumbed to rain. Water on that hot tarmac surface, now covered with a coating of oil and rubber left by the racing machinery, provided the perfect ingredients for making a skid pan. The cars slid about as if on ice and with no grip, the stopping distances were greatly increased, so consequently there were quite a few incidences of minor bumping and plenty of spins, to all add to the excitement of the whole weekend. According to Bunny we were each paid 22/6d (£1. 12½p) and had our circuit entrance fees refunded, for our help given to the grateful organisers. The journey back to Nairobi was very wet indeed, with the rain getting heavier as the storm increased its velocity and drenched the parched land. So much for Nairobi being called the city in the sun! However, it was the first long bout of rain that we had to endure. One should be thankful for that, and always remember that the mountains will have a direct effect on the weather.

Chapter 10

The Great Rift Valley

I stood on the edge of the escarpment with my fellow travellers, Frank Rothera, Ian Priddin and Andrew (Bunny) Todd. Like the early European explorers of comparative recent years, circa 1890s, we stood in wonderment on the lip of that immense chasm, which just opened up before us without any warning. We had not walked like those initial explorers but had driven about 30 miles northwest out from Nairobi. Nevertheless it was still a shock to experience the abruptness with which the 'Great African Rift Valley' appeared as if from nowhere. I gazed down the nearly precipitous scrub covered slope to the vast savannah plain some 2000 ft below, which stretched as far as the eye could see to the north and to the south. The cliff just seemed to go on into the distance in a straight line, very unusual for natural phenomena. Beneath us the yellowish parched grasslands of the savannah, extended 30 miles to the opposite western parallel wall of the valley, which rose out of the bluish heat haze in the distance. I had read about it, I had been taught about it at school, by a very enthusiastic geography master by the name of Gerald Elloy, and I had seen pictures and films of it. But nothing however, could even remotely prepare me for the occasion to have actually looked out over Africa's Great Rift Valley, one of the great natural wonders of the world.

Frank broke the silence by saying that no matter how often a person viewed that scene he was always impressed. He also pointed out that this was the place at which John Gregory, a prominent Scottish Geologist, first observed the great rift. Gregory fervently agreed with the theories of the Viennese geologist Eduard Suess, of the probability of a large scar valley stretching from the Arabian Peninsula through East Africa to Mozambique. Suess, although he never visited Africa, had worked out his theory using the maps made by cartographers with information gathered from the explorers and Arab trade caravans. Even though those first maps were remarkably accurate, not one of the early explorers actually recognised that the valley, which lay before us, was part of the natural occurrence of a fault line scarring the earth for 4000 miles.

Dr Livingstone made his discovery of lake Nyasa (Malawi) in 1859, and then German explorers Fisher and Baumann, at different times, pushed on into the area of the Rift, known in those days as Masailand, which was the territory of the very warlike Masai tribesmen. Joseph Thomson ventured further north, passing Lake Naivasha, always wary of the hostilities of the Masai and Kikuyu tribes ever in conflict over grazing territory, for both were nomadic and followed the rains with their cattle. Other explorers of the land up to and into the Ethiopian Highlands discovered a series of lakes and valleys seemingly linked together.

As a geologist, Gregory was sent out by the British Museum to join a poorly planned expedition across Somalia, which failed after only six weeks. He had though had a taste of the problems that could be encountered and was still ardently keen to explore that scar valley. All of this added foundation to encourage Gregory to mount his own expedition. So he set out northwest from Mombasa, to follow the ancient Arab caravan routes trekking into the interior. He was strongly discouraged by the few Europeans at Mombasa, because the terrain was very difficult and desolate and the natives were extremely hostile. The story went on to relate the comments of the two officials who accompanied the 'balding, lanky Scotsman, on the first part of the journey with the words "Will he nae come back again?"

The great valley splits near Lake Turkana (formally Lake Rudolf) in the northern territory of Kenya. The western leg continues southward through a series of lakes and depressions to Lake Tanganyika, one of the world's biggest lakes holding 1/6th of the fresh water on earth. However it was the eastern and most dramatic main trunk of the valley, which was to be Gregory's destination for his geological survey. His intention was to make for Lake Navashia, but there were particular difficulties of Masai belligerence at that time, (they were attacking not only other tribes but caravans and travellers also.) Gregory wisely moved on to do his first cross section survey of the valley at Lake Baringo a hundred miles to the north.

His work confirmed that the great scar valley was not caused by the normal erosion forces of temperature, wind and water, but by the enormous forces generated deep below the earth's surface by the movements of the tectonic plates tearing apart the earth's crust and causing the giant trench down the east side of Africa. And so it became known as Gregory's Rift. He had always reckoned that the Great African Rift Valley could be seen from the moon, a fact since verified by N.A.S.A.

As we drove down the steep escarpment road to start our exploration of that section of the Rift Valley, we were reminded of the close proximity of volcanic activity along the line of the rift. Most of the old giant volcanoes were long since dead, of which the Ngorongoro crater in the Serengeti Plain was probably the best known to us. Nevertheless, thirty active or semi active volcanoes, along with bubbling soda encrusted lakes and steam vents were sure signs of the continuing volcanic activity and rifting in that awesome place. In the northern Danakil desert of Ethiopia during 1960, a volcanic effusion eruption filled the crater of Erta-ale with a rare lava lake, whilst in 1966 an explosive eruption blew the top off the 9443 ft mountain of Ol-Doinyo Lengai (the Masai 'Mountain of God') on the border of Tanzania. Black lava poured out of the 2000 ft cone and black ash was pumped 25000 ft up into the skies for three weeks.

However, the alkaloid lava turned white as the moisture in the air chemically reacted with it and produced white sodium carbonate (washing soda) giving the whole mountain a bizarre winter like appearance. Both of those eruptions were very recent in the geological time scale, and so we were left with a real sense of journeying into unknown and primeval territory. We made several trips down into the rift, so I take the liberty of using 'poetic licence' to tell the story of *our* exploration of the African Rift Valley. Actually we only covered about 150 miles from Lake Nakuru in the North to Lake Magadi in the south, nevertheless that section was certainly one of the most dramatic parts of the Great Rift Valley that any one could encounter.

-0-0-0-0-0-0-0-0-0-0-0-0-0-0-0-0-0-0-0-0-0-0-0-0-0-0-0-0-0-0-

Lake Nakuru

Our travels had already taken us to Lake Nakuru at the time of our motor sport weekend, so hopefully I won't repeat myself too much! However, I wish to draw the connection of Lake Nakuru with the other two rift lakes, which we visited on our journey. That link was flamingos. Those pinkish white birds are the only animals to have the unique ability of living on the caustic waters of the volcanic soda lakes, which are fatal to most living creatures. The flamingos feed from the algae and crustaceans of these corrosive alkaline waters and usually stay paddling about in the waters day and night as a protection against predators looking for an easy meal. These birds take on the pink appearance, not from the red dust like the elephant does, but from the chemicals in the caustic soup in which they live. Flamingos away from these lakes revert to the normal white appearance, which causes problems for zoos and safari parks whose visitors expect to see 'pink flamingos'. They overcome this by feeding them a special diet!

One of the other remarkable characteristics of the flamingo is their courtship which is an unbelievably noisy affair coupled with an almost tribal dance ritual, as if performed on mass by some gigantic creature with a million legs. Even though they sometimes build nests on this and other lakes for some mysterious reason they migrate southwards to mate and lay their eggs on the remote vast soda lake of Natron just over the border in Tanzania. They build from the caustic mud a 'mini volcano' and perch their egg in the cone on top. The eggs are usually well protected, as very few animals will venture out into the immense heat and hostile nature of those caustic mud flats. A lone hyena or a desperate jackal has been known to venture out but only where the mud was dried hard by the unrelenting sun and the nests were relatively close to the edge of this unforgiving lake. If trapped in the mud, the corrosive solution would eat away the fir and flesh of the helpless creature, just leaving bleached bones as evidence of their reckless action.

Leslie Brown was the Kenyan government agricultural official in the fifties and tried to ascertain whether the long lake of Natron was the actual breeding ground for the flamingoes. Even his wildfowling experience on the mudflats of the Scottish estuaries did not prepare him for the ardours of trying to walk across those hellish conditions. He almost lost his life for, when struggling to return to the safety of the shoreline, the heat and fumes weakened him, while the corrosive cocktail burnt through his boots and attacked the flesh on his legs. Brown made the shoreline but still had a 7 mile walk back to his camp and Land Rover, and then a 45 mile drive back to the soda mining works at Magadi. He spent several weeks in hospital and vowed never to venture on to those soda flats again.

The flamingo nests were vulnerable to the flooding of the lake when rare heavy rains swamped the region and thousands of nests were washed away by the rising floodwaters, which followed some seasons of drought. In 1962 the beleaguered flamingo population attempted to nest on the adjacent Lake Magadi to the north. The soda concentration was even stronger than that of Natron and an ecological disaster was starting to happen when the lake dried out even more than usual. Wildlife photographers Alan and Joan Root found that the chicks' legs were becoming encrusted with the setting soda deposits and they were unable to move. With some help they broke away the 'concrete anklet' with a hammer but the process was too slow. Fortunately the East African Wildlife Society, the World Wild Life Fund and the British army quickly got involved, and at least 10,000 chicks were saved from that shimmering hellscape, but thousands more died. So when our journey through the Rift Valley started at Nakuru, it was good to see that the flamingo colonies had rejuvenated and the birds continued to traverse up and down the rift valley to the different lakes.

Because Lake Nakuru was known as the home of flamingoes it was easy to forget that the whole area, being a national park, was also a haven for hundreds of species of other birds. The toxicity varied around the lake depending upon the streams feeding the lake and other factors, so some fish were able to survive in those conditions in part of the lake. The parading marabou stork, which we had encountered at the kill in the game park, were particularly eyeing up the young flamingoes, and just awaiting an opportunity to stampede the flock so that they could take their choice of easy pickings. As we surveyed that amazing site I realised with a little sadness that every creature that we observed was part of a gigantic food chain, for every living thing has to eat, and it was sometimes difficult to appreciate that that was the natural law of the jungle.

-0-0-0-0-0-0-0-0-0-0-0-0-0-0-0-0-0-0-0-0-0-0-0-0-0-0-0-0-0-

Lake Naivasha

When we had descended the escarpment, the good road easily ran along the flat bottom of the valley. At different points it seemed to compete with the single track railway for the same piece of ground as we crossed and then re-crossed the line, both heading in the same direction to Naivasha and then Nakuru. There the railway branched off to continue to the north or to the west and Uganda. It did not seem to be long before we arrived at Lake Naivasha, which was considered by many to be the most beautiful lake in the Rift Valley. It was a complete contrast, predominantly a fresh water lake and not a soda lake like its neighbours. This was because it was fed by fresh streams from the mountains and volcanic catchments area all around and also had some sort of underground outlet at its southern end. Hence water loss was not all by evaporation, so that the soda, sulphur and other volcanic cocktails did not build up in their concentration.

That lush green oasis in that barren landscape seemed to me to be surrounded, almost cupped by the hills. On the west side, the Mau Escarpment formed the one wall of the Rift Valley, while to the north the buttresses of the long extinct volcanoes of the Eburu range, with the main peak of Ol-Doinyo Opuru reaching 9365 ft, appeared as a barrier to the north. To the east, the Ilkinangop Plateau, which rose to the Aberdare Mountains, made the other wall of the Rift Valley, whilst looking to the south, the large green mass of the active volcano Longonot seemed to block the outlet of the lake from the south end. Lake Naivasha is the highest lake in the Rift Valley at 6200 ft whilst, at the southern end, the valley falls away relatively gently by some 5000 ft to the austere Lake Magadi 120 miles away.

After the harsh scrub and parched savannah prevalent on our journey up the Rift Valley, I was amazed by the abundance of papyrus and sedge grasses along with water lilies and types of foliage too numerous to mention which covered the area around the lake. We were told that the slightly cooler air in the mornings, even slight frosts had been known, leave a more moist climate so that vegetation thrives.

Trees such as the flat topped acacia, supply nesting and lookout posts for what was considered to be the largest colony of fish eagles in Africa. The lake teams with fish, which attracts herons and colourful kingfishers, with hundreds of other birds creating what is thought to be

Africa's finest aviary. Fleets of pelicans arrived, to trawl for the fish recently introduced to try to combat the mosquito problem, the main source of malaria in the tropics. Close to the lake stood a clump of big trees, from which the bark seemed to be peeling off to reveal the body of the tree which glistened bright yellow in the sunlight, an unhealthy look. These were called by the early settlers 'fever trees', because of the association with malaria. Little did they know at that time, it was the mosquito, which was the culprit. Those trees were a type of acacia, which liked plenty of water, so tended to thrive in the same habitat as the mosquito. On such a lovely calm day it was difficult to imagine the rainy season, but of course we were way up in the mountains where the weather can take on a different perspective. We heard stories about the ferocity of a storm as it descended on the high winds from the mountains around, and turned the normally calm lake into a maelstrom of black fury, with hail stones the size of golf balls and the ensuing rain like the torrent of a waterfall.

We watched and waited, but were not patient enough to see a fish eagle take a large fish out of the lake whilst in full flight. The call of those beautiful bronze and white birds, which almost seemed to have the appearance of a black and white creature, certainly reminded me of the 'Sound of Africa'. The eerie, spine tingling flute-like whistling of those eagles, with the contrasting calls of the male and female, was the sound often unmistakably used in films to depict the wilds of Africa. We also saw some 5 ft goliath herons, the largest herons in the world, waiting more patiently than us, for a fish to swim into position; they as usual were well camouflaged from the water amongst the papyrus. Their diminutive cousins, along with a profusion of colourful little birds, all added to the experience of Lake Naivasha.

At the southern end the dense papyrus and towering sedge screened off the hippopotami, whose grunts and snorting told us they were there. We were even more cautious than at Hippo Pool in the Nairobi Game Park, as there was no steep drop down to the lake. Also we did not know if crocodile were in that lake too! I looked southwards towards Longonot and the narrow pass that seemed to open up between the volcano and the escarpment wall. That was surely where the secret outfall of water from the lake must go, as the underground stream seeped its way through the volcanic strata and underground mysteries on its way to Lake Magadi. I almost expected to see the explorer Joseph Thomson, or indeed John Gregory himself, come striding up towards Lake Naivasha after negotiating that narrow gorge, which was known by the very appropriate name of 'Hells Gate'!

-0-0-0-0-0-0-0-0-0-0-0-0-0-0-0-0-0-0-0-0-0-0-0-0-0-0-0-0-0-0-0-

Hells Gate

Hells Gate. The very name conjured up so many different ideas to the imagination of the soul. I had always been led to believe that an open mind was important, and the experiences of the journey and the African trip certainly confirmed that viewpoint. So it was not without a little trepidation that we set out to explore the gorge known as Hells Gate. We knew that it would get hot, as hot as hell they said, so this time we went prepared with food and drink, much to Ian's satisfaction. Frank's friend, Dave Wells, by now a friend to the four of us, arrived at the Rotheras' bungalow in his Land Rover along with a 'guide', Peter, a mutual friend of Frank and Dave, who joined us for this special trip.

We worked our way northwards again, but on this occasion instead of taking the escarpment road which descended into the Rift Valley, the Land Rover took us further up through the forests of the Kikuyu Escarpment, to the little plateau of the Kamuea Plain and the settlement of South Kinangop which nestled close to Mount Khingop, in the Aberdare Mountain Range. It was here that the Sasamua Dam had been built to create a small but necessary reservoir from which water was piped to the city of Nairobi some 60 miles south. I was surprised when we stopped at a native open-air market, which was set up on the edge of the local grassy airfield. We could see the windsock fluttering in the gentle breeze, but evidently, there was not much air traffic about. The market was a very colourful affair selling, or in reality bartering, for the mainly homegrown produce on offer. We obtained some sugarcane, which we were told was freshly cut that morning, to add to our picnic. "As a sweet" some bright spark reckoned.

The temperature was slowly rising. It would be a hot day; too hot to venture down into Hells Gate for a couple of hours, so we had our picnic, then ventured up closer to Mount Khingop in order to see the views. The Land Rover certainly helped to cover the steep and difficult terrain more easily than if we had been in the VW, but even *it* was struggling for breath as the altitude increased, causing an effective loss of power to the engine; and it was getting hotter! In the cab of the Land Rover, I noticed a long interior rear view mirror with an instrument dial at each end. Both gauges read '11', the left dial being an altimeter showing '1100 ft' whilst the right one showed 110 deg. fahrenheit. I was very bemused by the fact that it could be so hot so high. We were told that was why we had waited for the heat of midday to pass, before descending to explore the gorge down in the Rift Valley. It was even hotter down there!

The views were quite remarkable, and but for the heat haze, we could have seen a long way. Even so, it was an experience to be that high up, and I realized that was the highest point on earth that I had been to. We headed back off the mountain across the Ilkinangop Plateau to the escarpment and descended into The Great Rift Valley picking up the trail from Lake Naivasha, down towards Hells Gate itself.

As soon as we left the greenery of the lake, the typical parched savannah grasslands opened up before us, punctuated only by the thorn tree variety of the popular acacia trees. With rare exceptions these seemed to be the only trees to be able to survive the arid plains of the Rift Valley. The road had in reality disappeared as we bounced along a rough track which seemed to keep disappearing itself. It was dusty too, in the usual fashion of the African country waiting for the rains, with the slightest breeze or animal movement kicking up the dry scorched earth. The cliffs of the western barrier appeared as if from nowhere to channel us down between the right hand wall and the volcano of Mount Longonot which dominated the eastern side to our left. An unusual feature of a distinct column of reddish rock, sticking up out of the plain like some prehistoric phallic symbol, added mystery to the whole environment. Our guide pointed this out as Fischer's Column, named after the German explorer Gustav Fischer who discovered Hells Gate. This was the lava plug of rock left over from a small extinct volcano, long since worn away by the elements of wind and rain.

The region was a haven for wildlife. Birds and mammals were said to be most prolific in that area of the Rift Valley. Small birds and a species of swift nesting in the cliffs searched for the numerous insects, whilst still on the wing, an eagle glided along the cliff face, oblivious to being buzzed by the defensive swifts. A secretary bird, as usual on the ground, strutted about on its 2 ft legs on the lookout for a lizard, or more hopefully a snake. They looked on any variety of snakes as a delicacy, and seemed oblivious as to whether it was poisonous or not. The secretary bird, tensed up like a coiled spring waiting to jump aside or up into the air, was so quick that it inevitably avoided the strike of the snake. Before the snake had recovered to strike again, the bird had used the talons of its very strong legs to beat several fatal blows on to the reptile.

Thomson's gazelle along with other antelope and prairie grazers were spied in the distance, whilst the cliffs too were home to another unusual mammal, known locally as a dassie or rock hyrax. These looked a bit like a rabbit with a short snout, perhaps a marmot? Actually they belonged to neither family but were unique. I couldn't really believe that they were related to the large elephant! This was typical of Africa. All these animals therefore encouraged the predators to be in attendance; big cats such as lion, leopard and cheetah prowled the rift along with their smaller cousins. I had hoped particularly to see some of these rare cats. The beautiful tanned coat caracals, about the size of a Labrador, with long hairy ears, the more well known lynx with its grey tabby appearance, the small ocelots and jungle cats too were present, but so well camouflaged that we knew that six 'noisy' people would never find them. Nevertheless like the lions from the game park, I am sure that they saw us too!

A small pack of pie-dogs, or African wild dogs, wandered about in the searing heat searching for something edible. These were not feral dogs but a breed in their own right and could be treacherous if a person was on their own. Servals, jackals and of course hyenas were always about where a hunt might take place. The buzzards, soaring high on the thermals above the gorge, certainly added more than a touch of danger to our adventure as we alighted from the Land Rover, under the rise of another fault scarp cliff face which almost blocked our view of the volcano.

We must have been a few miles from Lake Naivasha by this time, for the land took on a wilder and more desolate appearance. Clumps of lava and rocky outcrops, partly covered by volcanic ash, hardened by the action of sun and rain, broke up the level savannah plain. Another tower of rock, which harboured some vegetation growth on the top, was called by the Masai tribesmen Embarta, (The Horse). It just rose out of the ground like a sentinel guarding a mysterious location. In the distance I was sure that I spotted wisps of smoke, not just one, but also several just seemed to appear then disappear. I hoped that they were not a prairie fire, for in that environment with the dried grasslands it would spread disastrously quickly. "Don't worry" said our guide, "its just the 'devil in Hells Gate' getting ready to greet us". A troop of baboons sauntered through the parched grass, in the formation of a platoon of soldiers, ready to defend the females and young ones in the centre from any attack, as they made their way to the protection of the cliffs.

Suddenly a deep ravine opened up amid the arid scrubland. Dave and Peter our guide indicated for us to keep quiet, as we looked down into the thick vegetation of the abyss into which we were to descend. This was weird. A rift valley in the Rift Valley. The parched desolation of the area littered with rock and patches of black volcanic lava contrasted sharply with the thick jungle growing down in the ravine. I realised now that the illusion of smoke in the distance was in fact steam, arising from out of the ground. We followed an almost indistinguishable path over the edge of the cliff and down the steep uneven animal track into the ravine. Then we worked our way slowly and as quietly as we could through thick vegetation, which provided cover for the many unknown creatures aware that we had ventured into their territory.

I was mesmerised by the colourful array of large butterflies flitting about in the shrubbery and wondered what else was lurking there, out of view. It was very hot, but a different heat. Not the dry searing heat of the savannah above, but a humid heat, for the ravine was damp with the foliage holding as much moisture as it could to support the mini jungle. We were all sweating profusely and not just from the heat. The unknown of what could be loitering in the undergrowth caused a nervous sweat as well. Peter was in the lead with Dave, who carried a gun for use only in an emergency, and the four of us pursued in single file along the twisting, difficult to follow, trail deeper into the mysterious chasm.

The procession stopped suddenly. Evidently a cobra was sunning itself on an open part of the path. I think I was relieved that the snake had decided to slither into hiding before I got to that point, but on reflection, it would have been interesting to actually see the reptile in its natural habitat. The six intrepid explorers continued ever deeper into the gorge. My imagination at one time counted seven travellers as the sweat ran down into my eyes and blurred my vision. It was getting hotter, and with the steamy columns seeming to be getting ever closer, the smell of sulphur and rotten eggs added to the drama. Sometimes we walked on banks of eroded volcanic ash, at other times on patches of exposed lava showing the flow patterns cast indefinitely into the volcanic rock.

At one point our attention was held by the black smooth rock of glazed glass, obsidian, formed by the extreme pressure and heat underground, that lay at the edge of a lava flow vented out of a fissure. This was lethal stuff for where broken the fixed shards of 'glass', like some primitive defensive weapon of the gate, could cut to pieces anything that came into contact with it. These features had not necessarily come from eruptions from the volcano Longonot, but from the cracks and fissures caused by the constant movements of the subterranean forces. It was here that the Earth's crust was very thin and the volcanic action was very close to the surface.

The ground rattled and shook in a most disturbing way. The issue of boiling mud and water gurgling out of reddish tinged holes in the rock and spouting steam up into the atmosphere made it an awesome place. It rumbled and hissed like some great ancient monster trying to escape from Gehenna. The smell of sulphur crowded out other smells, which would also have been exhumed from out of the bowels of the Earth. The ground rock was too hot to touch and would have I am sure started to melt our footwear, if we had lingered. I could feel the heat through my· boots! This was Dante's Inferno. This was Hells Gate and it conjured up every thought that any one could have about the entrance to hell.

We arrived back at the Land Rover tired and thirsty, having walked about three miles in the searing heat of the gorge. I wondered what the heat would have been like if we had descended earlier when it was even hotter! Even so, Frank still reckoned that the temperature was something horrific, and apart from the humid relief of the mini jungle, it was the dust and fumes, added to the heat, that made the expedition something for us to remember for the rest of our lives. Frank caught my gaze up at Longonot as it emerged from behind the scar cliff, to dominate and control the area known as Hells Gate. I had always had a fascination with mountains, and must have looked upon the peak with the longing of a mountaineer. "We will climb that volcano soon" said Frank "but don't forget that it is still active!" On the way back home we talked about an assault on the 9000 ft plus volcano of Mount Longonot and the opportunity to look down into the crater of one of the Rift's volcanoes. We were certainly gluttons for punishment, for we had covered another 150 miles round trip. We were definitely seeing Kenya.

-0-0-0-0-0-0-0-0-0-0-0-0-0-0-0-0-0-0-0-0-0-0-0-0-0-0-0-0-0-

Mount Longonot

We agreed to tackle Mount Longonot. Having survived the descent into the depths of Hells Gate, the next obvious venture was to climb the volcano, so we decided to set off early morning, in order to do the ascent before the heat of midday made it too exhausting. We were supposed to be fit and young anyway, but this would certainly test us out. We turned left off the tarmac escarpment road by the railway level crossing where both the road and railway seem to squeeze through the narrow gap between Longonot and the eastern escarpment wall of the Rift Valley. We were pleased that we didn't have to travel too long on the rough trail. Not that we did not like traversing dirt roads, but we did not wish to damage the VW that had served us so well on our explorations. Dirt roads were one thing but very rough tracks were another. The vista of the mountain took on a different appeal as we approached closer to the cone of the volcano. With a beckoning, which seemed to come from a living thing, we felt drawn to climb up to the top.

"Only 2000 ft to the summit" called out Frank, who reminded us that we were already at 7000 ft, so we only had to climb a quarter of the mountain on that occasion. Frank's logic came to the fore again.

Ian, Frank and I left our pullovers along with our picnic in the car, for it was quite chilly when we set out from the bungalow soon after sunup. Bunny however decided to keep his on. After only a short walk through the endless savannah grasses, we started up the north side of the mountain. The going was not too steep or difficult but nevertheless we were pleased to have made an early start. The temperature was starting to climb, as we climbed up the side of the mountain, although I presumed that it was really the effort needed which made us feel hot. Bunny's woolly was soon tied around his waist and the three of us were gloating over the fact that we had decided not to wear ours!

I was amazed by how much of the scrub up the side of the volcano was actually small trees, which seemed to just cling on to the steep ground. They certainly helped when vertical sections had to be scaled, for even though we followed a kind of path it was, as is often the case in the mountains, difficult to track. It took us about a couple of hours to reach the rim of the crater, for the last few hundred feet had been difficult over steep and loose ground but being four keen lads we had to reach the actual summit. The rim was not truly symmetrical with the section to our right climbing on upwards to a fixed marker pole embedded into a large block of concrete. It has always amazed me that people seem to have a fixation about carting heavy things to the tops of mountains.

I peered into the crater with very mixed feelings. The rim fell away quite steeply to start with before dropping in a seemingly vertical fall to the crater floor way below us. This was not just a normal mountain of rock and meagre soil giving support to the hardy vegetation living almost parasitically on its slopes. This mountain gave me the impression that it was alive. The scrub and diminutive trees were in contrast to the dried yellowish grasses on the floor of the Rift Valley, and the floor of the crater seemed to be even richer in foliage than the slopes of the volcano. Yes, that was the difference, this mountain was a volcano and even though it was considered by some people to be dormant, I felt that Longonot was a light sleeper. It was without doubt breathing, for the patches of cloud floating about in the mile wide floor of the crater were not the early morning mist still not evaporated by the sun, but vents of steam breathed out from deep under ground by that slumbering unpredictable giant. I was sure that it was at least another 2000 ft down to the bottom of the crater and wondered if one did venture down into that awesome pit, what prehistoric wildlife would be found!

The views back to the north were stunning. Although the heat haze was starting to dim the horizon there were still good views of Lake Naivasha along with the mountains and escarpment walls of the Rift which all emphasised that unique place in East Africa. To the west the scar cliffs and entrance to Hells Gate chasm, could be made out, and I could see how the lay of the land would have channelled some vast ancient river from an immense Lake Naivasha down through the gorge of Hells Gate and on to the lower part of the Rift Valley to another lake in the distance. To the south, the Great African Rift Valley reached way across the savannah, housing the soda lakes of Magadi and Natron on its journey southwards between the plateau of the Serengeti and Africa's highest mountain, Kilimanjaro. It was approaching 11 o'clock, with the heat of the day not quite at its maximum and with only light patchy cloud around to shield us from the relentless sun, we felt it prudent to start our descent. No going down into the crater on this occasion. I was intrigued by the black clouds way in the distance to the south. Perhaps down there they were experiencing a big tropical storm. Perhaps we should return back to the car for these storms can travel very quickly!

(During my research for verification of place names and other relevant and to me interesting information, I discovered that the volcano Ol-Doinyo Lengai called by the Masai 'The Mountain of God' explosively erupted in August 1966. Although first spotted by airline pilots on the 14th August, being in a very remote part of the Rift Valley, it did not attract worldwide news interest. The eruption was monitored and by the morning of the 23rd August had virtually ceased. However on the 1st September 1966 another violent ash eruption was reported. On 3rd and 4th September the eruptions continued with ash fall reported as far north as the southern edge of Lake Magadi. It is interesting to note that the black clouds, that we saw to the south, were not rain clouds at all but the ash column from the violent eruption of Ol-Doinyo Lengai, for the date we climbed Mount Longonot was 2nd September 1966).

The descent back down the cone of the volcano was accomplished a lot quicker than the ascent. The first part enabled us to practise the old art of scree running, where balance and a strong head were needed as we slid like a skier without skis down the loose volcanic dirt on the side of the mountain. When the vegetation was reached, a more civilized descent was usually made without the endless stops required on our ascent to overcome the exertion caused by heat and altitude.

Back at the car we found that the VW had been broken into. Weird really, as we had seen no one since we had turned off the main road some hours earlier. Frank, Ian and I each had lost our pullovers and we soon discovered that our picnic lunch was missing, along with an umbrella. Bunny, the ever-cautious one, still had his. We were just about to depart when two members of the local constabulary appeared in a Land Rover, and I guessed that we should have had a look around for tyre tracks ourselves. Ian reported the theft and everyone mooched about looking for clues. I would have liked to look inside the Land Rover, but Frank, being more used to the ways of Africa, encouraged us to think of our loss as a parking fee and didn't want us to have a confrontation with the police, especially as they were armed. He later admitted that they probably had stolen our items.

So we retired back to Naivasha town for some lunch and another look at the souvenir shops with their wooden carvings of African animals and peoples. On our way back to the Rothera's home we again followed the now familiar route up the side of the Kikuyu escarpment but this time in daylight. I was impressed by the range of pretty green hills, some thirty miles away, rising up above the eastern wall of the Rift Valley where they just seemed to stretch onwards. The hills and mountains of that part of Kenya always seemed to have green vegetation, a lovely contrast to the dried grasslands of the plains. "That is good Safari Rally country and leads into the Ngong hills", commented Frank, and I guessed that was another expedition he had planned for us.

At the top of the escarpment were a small group of natives with a roadside stall selling souvenirs. We had not seen these folks before, however Frank had! "Do you want to see how fast these guys can run?" said Frank with a mischievous laugh. Some ran to the car with a selection of goods, but when they were near, Frank drove on a bit then slowed down, as they approached, he drove on again. After a few times I began to feel sorry for the native lads, indeed we all did, so when Frank did stop he suggested that we ought to buy some goods, as the lads had certainly earned their money. We could certainly see why the Kenyan athletes were so good at distance running, and they were so used to altitude training too!

-0-0-0-0-0-0-0-0-0-0-0-0-0-0-0-0-0-0-0-0-0-0-0-0-0-0-0-0-0-

Lake Magadi

Well, we just had to try them didn't we? I mean the 'Safari Rally' roads round the Ngong Hills. Great dirt roads and fantastic scenery in abundance; it all quite reminded me of mid Wales without the tarmac lanes. I still couldn't get over how green the hills were, such a contrast to the bush, but mountains and hills do seem to have the ability to attract the moisture so absolutely necessary for any kind of life. Like all the mountains of the Rift Valley, they were a series of old volcanic peaks eroded by eons of time into the rounded hills of the Ngong range. We just so enjoyed driving through one of the most picturesque parts of Kenya on completely traffic free smoothish dirt roads; absolutely fantastic.

It was not too long before we found ourselves on the main dirt road to Magadi where we were faced with a sign indicating that the journey to Magadi was not to be undertaken lightly. It was 46 miles to the lake on a rough unsurfaced road. There was no petrol, or hotel, or café there, just the soda extraction plant and a few buildings that had been around for many years. A brief discussion ensued. We had ¾ tank of petrol, (Franks estimate), food and water, thanks to Ian and four young men with a thirst for adventure. "It will be very, very hot", said Frank "but I can get some petrol from the works by the lake. Just keep an eye out for missing bridges and the Masai tribesmen, for it's their territory we're going into!" Without too much deliberation we decided to continue to drive onwards to that awesome area which holds, and was considered by many people to be, the two most inhospitable lakes in the world. We would visit Lake Magadi, the first of those two corrosive sumps of water and soda, lying nearly 5000 ft below and 120 miles south of Lake Naivasha.

The green foliage had disappeared, to be replaced by the scrub and parched dry grasslands of the endless savannah stretching as far into the distance as the eye could see. We were descending to the

Olekemonge Plain on the main dirt road, which changed its characteristic without warning. A relatively smooth gravel surface suddenly dropped into a dried up riverbed covered in broken concrete, which made it possible to ford through the river if it was not too deep! Signs of the remnants of a bridge were in evidence but the steel and wood were much more valuable to the Masai than to those drivers on their way to Magadi. The course of the riverbed ran from the hills that we had just traversed and Frank gave us an interesting dilemma. The river was dried up now and we crossed over via the concrete ramps, which saved us from getting bogged down in sand. However if it rained in the hills, then a flash flood would race through the watercourse, meaning that when we returned we might have to wait for the water level to subside. That could take some time depending on the severity of the storm. None of us could remember a weather forecast, but they were a bit hit and miss anyway.

Anthills, some 6–8 ft tall were another part of that ever-changing landscape. Usually enveloping a thorn tree for support, they beckoned with a morbid curiosity for us to investigate. Caution was, as always needed, for we didn't know what other creatures might be around, apart from the odd anteater of course. The hills were made of the red soil mud, which had hardened to provide the structure, housing the whole colony of ants. There were many, many species, most not dangerous but a big nuisance if in the wrong place as some could soon destroy a wooden building. There were only a few around, perhaps about 1 inch or so in length. A number of ants could be quite large!

We had already seen some giraffe and various antelope when we spotted more of the little Thomson's gazelles who had broke from the cover of a small clump of acacia trees as we approached. Then as the track rounded a hillock, with scarps of basalt, the black volcanic rock, rising some 50 ft or more to our right we spotted some native mud huts neatly arranged in a circle and surrounded by a boma, a thick hedge of thorn tree branches. We got out of the car to take the mandatory photographs. None of us noticed them at first, they had just appeared as if from nowhere. Two Masai moran, or warriors.

Well I assumed that they were morans by their attire. Red ochre robes loosely draped over one shoulder hid the tall, thin but muscular bodies of these men. Their shiny jet-black hair, knotted and greased with animal fat, shone in the sunlight and gave them a very distinctive appearance, but it was their long broad pointed spears that seized my attention. Frank gestured for us to get back into the car. There were four of us and only two of them (as far as we knew), but we all felt that in a confrontation we would not stand a chance, these guys were trained warriors and not to be messed with. The older one approached Frank in the drivers seat and began to make demands. It was good that Frank was able to argue with them in Swahili, although we had made one fatal mistake of not closing the windows even though it was getting very hot. The other one kept the three of us occupied by brandishing his spear through the open rear window of the VW. At least I got a very good close up look at the spear with it's long broad pointed blade which appeared to have been forged out of iron and sharpened to a keen edge. Perhaps it had been made from the steel from the missing bridge?

After a little while, as the banter between the Masai warrior and Frank got more excited, an agreement was reached. It would cost us 5 shillings (Kenyan currency) for the photos that we had taken of their village, or was it just a toll for using their road? We paid up and they waved us goodbye as we continued our journey. They were just guarding their cattle and had probably got a bit bored, for not many tourists ventured out into that part of the Rift Valley. We saw their large herd of cattle, which seemed to me to be quite scrawny, slightly humped at the shoulder and sporting a vicious pair of long sharp horns. These were the true nomadic Masai peoples who had for thousands of years guided their most prized possession, their cattle, to the pastures most suitable for them. Their grazing lands stretched way out down the Rift Valley to the crater plateau of the Serengeti in Tanzania and even far beyond that. They knew nothing of boundaries marked on a map by the European colonial occupiers of recent times. It was all their territory with their right to traverse, fought for in many tribal conflicts over the centuries. They appeared to me to be proud and traditional peoples who had lived and worked with nature for generations, not upsetting the fragile ecosystem that such a harsh environment could support. They were just as important a part of that system as the animals that they shared the savannah with. It had certainly been an interesting encounter.

We came across a sign indicating only a mile to the Oldauau gorge archaeological site, considered by some experts to be the oldest prehistory stone age site in the world. True, that site had been located on the edge of a very large lake or inland sea, complimented by the bigger version of Lake Naivasha to the north. It took a lot of imagination to try to picture the life of those early peoples living there by the waters of a great lake long since gone. There were signs of many archaeological digs scattered about the place, but I think it was the unusual thatched, little white circular stone hut that captured our imagination, for it was the only building there. We thought it was the office or whatever but it turned out to be the loo!

I was amazed by the number of scarp ridges sticking up out of the ground, which sometimes seemed to lean on to each other in a ripple effect reaching 100 ft high. This was further evidence of much rifting in the Rift Valley itself. Even so, we still made our way through that remote and awesome country, always descending into the deepest, and as we would soon find out, hottest parts of that relentless gigantic trench trying to tear Africa apart. And it was getting hotter and hotter; I thought it was just as well that we did not have a thermometer, we could only speculate!

Finally as we descended by yet another fault scar, we spied the weird sight of the peculiar pink apparition of the Magadi soda lake. The vast soda encrustations gave me the impression of decayed icing buckling on a gigantic cake in an open oven. As we approached closer, the acrid smell of soda with that caustic cocktail, fouled our nostrils and I could almost feel the fumes hanging in the air affecting my breathing. The searing heat from above bounced back again off the expanse of pink-white crystals, while the overpowering midday sunlight reflected off those soda flats with an intensity of light that I had never experienced before. I was sure that without eye protection we would soon have been suffering from Magadi's version of snow blindness. The soda was not so much brought down by the streams from the volcanic ash on the hills around, but was and still is actually forced upwards by the relentless geothermal activity in the not so very deep down, red hot vitals of the bowels in the earth itself. That activity constantly bubbling up a thick caustic concoction into that hostile lake, along with the intense tropical heat could cause the temperature to often reach 150 deg F. It was the combined effects of all these occurrences, which nurtured the shimmering hellscape of Lake Magadi.

No wonder that there was nobody about, for 'only mad dogs and Englishmen go out in the midday sun' and there was not even any dog, never mind any living creature, about there anyway. The small township based around the Magadi Soda Company seemed deserted. The sign was right. No petrol station, no hotel and certainly no café! For who, apart from those who had to, through work, would want to visit such a place in such a forbidding and desolate part of the world. Well we were there and the first job was to get some petrol before attempting to gather information about the area. We headed for the station yard and found a large galvanized building which, according to the dilapidated sign above the door was the workshop of the Magadi Soda Company. Outside stood two ancient petrol pumps rusting away, like everything round about, from the caustic atmosphere prevalent at Magadi. One of the pumps inferred petrol whilst the other was obviously diesel from the stains and spillage at its base. Another sign said 'Not for Resale. Company Vehicles Only'. The big sliding door was partly open so we, or rather Frank wandered in, the temperature was horrendous with the vertical tropical sun beating mercilessly down on to the tin roof and with not a vestige of fresh air in the place. No wonder there was nobody about!

Now Frank just seems to have the ability to source whatever he wants, so we were not surprised when he located a native mechanic asleep outside in the limited shade at the back of the workshop. He should, we thought, have been on duty, for he assumed that Frank was a boss from the Soda Company. He quickly jumped to attention when Frank questioned him in Swahili about petrol and was within seconds filling the VW up with the precious liquid. At the edge of the little town, the track wound up a rise to a lone building overlooking the lake and the narrow peninsular running northwards alongside the edge of the lake to the terminal of the railway line and the loading dock for the soda ash. It was an isolated police post serving two purposes. The first was to try and keep track of any persons deemed mad enough to want to go on further southwards to the hot fresh water springs entering the water at the southern end of the lake. A phenomenon that I just could not understand. Where did the fresh water come from and why in that heat should there be a marsh at the southern end too?

To travel any further a Land Rover type vehicle was needed, filled with petrol and plenty of spare drinking water as well. There was basically not even much of a track to follow across the arid rifted ground littered with lava rock and obsidian, which blocked the way of any unwary traveller. Whilst it was only approximately twenty five miles or so to the Tanganyika (Tanzania) border and Magadi's bigger sister Lake Natron, with the Ngare Ngiro Swamp protecting the northern end and the active volcano Ol-Doinyo Lengai the southern end the difficult terrain just went on for a long, long way, thousands of square miles in fact. So the police posts main purpose was to also monitor the borderlands and record animal migration movements too. From that area the threatening thick dark clouds just distinguishable through the heat haze prompted our departure from that ominous place.

(As previously mentioned the volcano Ol-Doinyo Lengai had exploded just four days previous to our visit to Magadi. So those dark clouds were clouds of soda ash ejected during the eruption of the volcano. I now find it interesting that even the police post did not know of the eruption, so demonstrating the vast remoteness of that area).

Crossing back over the railway line in Magadi, I wandered about the location of a railway in such a wild part of Africa? Commercial reasons of course, for in 1909, when the soda lake was deemed to be a valuable mineral source, the only way to economically transport the soda ash was to build a 100 mile branch line to join with the then recently completed Mombasa to Lake Victoria railway. That was an engineering feat in itself, and was completed in 1913. Shortly after the First World War the railway became profitable and exports of soda often exceeded one million tons a year. The thirty square mile expanse of Lake Magadi was probably the only mine, mineral extract site in the world to have its resources refilled by nature, in fact the soda produced by the volcanic action beneath the surface was increasing faster than miners could extract it!

The journey back seemed to drag. The very hot dusty rough road was very wearisome, even to hardened travellers, for this journey was well over 200 miles and virtually all on dirt roads! When it started to rain we didn't know whether to welcome it or not, for we still had some wadi's to cross and when we got to the dried up river bed with the missing bridge, there was quite a torrent of water flowing through. We took a chance, for the water seemed to be continuing to rise and it would be dark in an hour or so. I along with my fellow explorers, was very relieved to get safely to the other side. However ,the driver could not relax, for the dirt road had in the wet taken on a very slippery condition and that too added to a day of extremes in what the tropical climate could demonstrate to us. To say that we were pleased to be home back at the Rothera's was an understatement. David and Edna Rothera were relieved, and then a little angry with us for not informing them where we were going. Our safety was their concern, for that country is so very different to gentle England. Where we had been was considered to be too remote and dangerous to have ventured, without informing our hosts as to where we were travelling. In the event of a break down or accident, people have not been found for weeks and most did not survive the combination of extreme temperatures, some hostile natives and hungry predators. We were told that we were very lucky!

-0-0-0-0-0-0-0-0-0-0-0-0-0-0-0-0-0-0-0-0-0-0-0-0-0-0-0-0-0-

What we had seen as we explored a short 150 mile section of the Great African Rift Valley on it's way through Kenya, was just a little of that gigantic African continent. If I hadn't seen them for myself the sights and places could have just seemed to have been conjured up in the pages of a science fiction novel. Each section had its own special attraction. The beautiful lakes of Naivasha and Nakuru showing their remarkable bird life: the drama of Hells Gate and the volcano Longonot: the forbidding and desolate beauty of Magadi and environs, all built in my mind memories, which would last a lifetime. I had read about it, I had been taught about it and then in 1966 I had the fortune to explore a dramatic part of it. Yes, the Great African Rift Valley certainly captivated my mind.

Chapter 11

The Lunatic Express

It had been arranged for the four avid explorers to travel to the ancient city of Mombasa at the edge of the Indian Ocean. A two centre holiday as it is called today. The big difference was that today holidaymakers, if they do travel inland to Nairobi from Mombasa, usually travel from one sanitised tourist resort to the modern hotels of the capital city by plane. At the time we intended to travel, the tarmac road only ventured a little way into the savannah scrub and torrid regions, at either end of our excursion, so we were encouraged to make that journey by train. The 330 miles, 14-hour trip we were assured, was a must for all devout African travellers. An experience we should take, to add to the adventures of our exploration of Kenya. Initially Ian and I were disappointed, as we wanted to experience a really long drive across those relentless bush lands. However the VW Beetle had now been handed back into the garage, which had kindly agreed to the delayed part exchange as arranged with Frank's father and both he and the garage seemed relieved that the Beetle had survived our adventures. Consequently it was deemed much more practical to travel by the over night train.

We packed for the beach holiday that we would now benefit from and I relished the chance to explore another part of Kenya and it's culture. What new exiting scenery and creatures might we find in Mombasa I wondered? Afternoon tea at the station hotel set us up in the proper frame of mind for our journey to the coast. We had to do things correctly travelling colonial style; although we could not afford the luxury of first-class travel we thought that second-class travel should be perfectly ok. Having boarded at 6.30, pm surviving the congestion around the notice boards informing travellers which carriage and compartment they were booked into, we settled into the spacious six berth sleeping compartment reserved for us. With a loud whistle the train departed from the station as it's clock chimed 7 o'clock. We all smiled while the sounds of a huge engine reverberated along the platform as the big English Electric diesel locomotive seemed to shoulder the load of a long, long train and coaxed the ensemble into motion. It was still light as the train meandered through the suburbs of Nairobi and under the railway bridge on the road near to the airport. The track now ran alongside the Nairobi National Park for a few miles and in the few moments of dusk, in the half-light between day and night, our imaginations certainly worked overtime with the friendly banter of trying to recognise the various animals in the game park. However it was soon dark, then an attendant ushered a young African man into the compartment. He had little choice as we had already commandeered the top four of the six bunks available but he didn't seem to mind, if fact he seemed to be a quiet, well educated young man who worked in Nairobi but was visiting his family north of Mombasa.

Dinner on the train was held in two sittings, we had opted for the later one at 8.30 pm, Frank considered it more civilised and less crowded and it didn't seem that long since tea anyway. We certainly ate very well during our stay in Kenya, but exploration of foreign lands definitely built hearty appetites, so by the time the bell clanked along the narrow corridor calling the second sitting diners for their meal, we were all feeling a bit peckish. I peered out of the compartment window to confirm my suspicions. The train was negotiating a long tight bend so one could see the engine with it's powerful spot lamp on the front looking for big game or obstructions, whilst one could also see the rear of the train following the curve of the track. Frank reminded me that, although the Kenyan railway had the narrower gauge of 1 metre, which enabled the rails curvature to bend tighter than the usual 3ft. 6in. found in Britain, the main reason was the availability of used rolling stock from India. This was in contrast to the 3ft. 6in. British system used in Egypt or South Africa.

The excellent meal was enjoyed in a very relaxed manner for we could have stayed, if we had wanted to, in the dining room, as the bar was open all night! Even so, after a couple of the local Tusker beers, we all adjourned back to our bunks to get a good nights sleep before sampling the delights of Mombasa. Our fellow traveller was fast asleep in one of the bottom bunks, all of which had been made up into comfortable beds by the attendants on the train; admirable service. A visit to the toilet is always necessary on any long journey, so we now found we had a choice of eastern or western facilities, providing of course that they were not occupied. A torch was recommended on a night time visit to the facilities, for lights did have a habit of going out at the most inappropriate time! Also useful, according to Frank, to make sure that nothing was trying to climb up the hole in the loo. The eastern cubicle at the end of each carriage was the usual flat ceramic tray with foot recesses so that the occupier could squat over the hole emptying directly on to the track. No u-bend as verified by the torch! At the beginning of the next carriage the western cubicle housed a normal English type toilet but also without the benefit of a u-bend, either type was comparatively noisy as the sounds of the train and drafts from beneath the carriage reverberated through the hole in the floor.

Ablutions completed, we all had a good look at the train from the window of the darkened compartment, trying to work out the various shapes and shadows cast by the moonlight over the vast savannah plain. It was quite impressive; for apart from the lights on the train, we could not see a single light anywhere out in the unknown. Ian asked Frank about what those two men at the bar were meaning by talking about the train being the 'Lunatic Express'. "Ah, um, it's a long story," said Frank, well knowing that we all loved long stories! So please bear with me as I will try to give a brief insight into the problems and story of the building of that railway across very difficult and dangerous terrain.

> *"What it will cost no words can express;*
> *What is its object no brain can suppose;*
> *Where it will start from no one can guess;*
> *Where it is going nobody knows.*
> *What is the use of it none can conjecture;*
> *What it will carry there's none can define;*
> *And in spite of George Curzon's superior lecture,*
> *It clearly is naught but a lunatic line."*

The above was the well publicized view of a member of the British parliament in the late nineteenth century, when support for the building of a railway system across Kenya from the coast to Lake Victoria and Uganda was envisaged. It would have had a two-fold purpose, first to open up the vast and relatively unknown interior of Africa, similar to what had been done in America and then India. (Although of course those railways followed the early settlers and pioneers of those countries, not leading them.) Second; to have access to Uganda and the source of the River Nile, particularly because of the British influence in Egypt at that time having control of the Suez Canal, being vital for the trade routes to India.

It was envisaged to also help in ending the slave trade still illegally operating in Africa. The actual project was finalised to extend from Mombasa, on the Kenyan Indian Ocean coast, to Lake Victoria and was expected to take some four to five years to complete, all paid for by the British taxpayer of course. There were seemingly endless arguments in the British Parliament about the wisdom of such an undertaking of building a railway into what was then a relatively unknown and hostile part of the world; hence the poem!

George Whitehouse was the engineer given the task of building that railway. When he arrived at the small coastal port of Mombasa in December 1895 he only had a sketch plan of the route the railway should take and little knowledge of the land, which it was to cross. What he learned would have sent many a lesser man back home to England. West of Mombasa lay the torrid waterless wasteland of the Taru Desert that most of the trade-slave caravan routes had avoided. Next lay 300 miles of scrub savannah, covered by the notorious thorn tree bushes, which teemed with lion and other predators and which also swarmed with tsetse fly and mosquito. The volcanic highlands, the home of the African Great Rift valley with it's 2000 ft escarpments had to then be negotiated, and the final 100 miles to the giant lake was said to be nothing less than a soggy quagmire. The story of the building of the 'Lunatic Express' was to be one of Africa's most vivid sagas.

The sleepy old town of Mombasa awakened to the building of the facilities necessary for the offloading of the tons of materials and multitude of construction workers essential for that huge project. Docks, warehouses and accommodation were needed and quickly built and immediately caused the problem of a lack of drinking water. Whitehouse solved this by damming a stream and building a dam and reservoir to house rainwater; also as there was no water for the first 100 miles of the route, he calculated that they would need to transport some 10,000 gallons per day!

Mombasa was of course on an island, so the first problem that Whitehouse encountered, was to bridge the Macupa Creek (sometimes spelt Makupa), this was done and eventually became the Macupa Causeway. In December 1896, a year after Whitehouse had arrived in Mombasa, just 23 miles of track had been laid. The Railway Committee, although acknowledging the difficult start to the project, were very unhappy about the time table, for at that rate of progress the first scheduled train would not happen until 1924!

Ronald Preston, the grandfather of rally driver Vic Preston who we met at the Nakuru racetrack, was a British engineer who arrived from India with experience of building railways there. He was given the job of overseeing the railhead, the plate laying of the track, and building whatever bridges or cuttings etc were needed to forge the railway ahead on its momentous journey. Sometimes a necessary diversion was taken to keep up the speed of construction insisted on by the Railway Committee. Materials and of course water were mainly freighted up from Mombasa by train on the track already laid, which served as the vital communication and supply line to the construction teams.

The Taru plain though, was a true taste of the problems that those incredible pioneers would have to endure. In the December over 500 workers were hospitalised in makeshift tents, suffering from the scourge of the tropical diseases of malaria, dysentery, tropical ulcers and pneumonia. In a few weeks half the workforce were immobilized. Work did continue over what had seemed initially to be quite reasonable terrain. However the razor sharp thorn bushes caused countless cuts and lacerations, which could easily turn into tropical ulcers, the red choking dust got everywhere and the temperature even at night rarely dropped below 100 deg F. The land had been described as "a thorn infested frying pan" and M.F. Hill states in his official history of the railway *"that it seemed as if the very spirit of Africa resented the intrusion of the white man's railway"*.

It was not just the workers who succumbed to the problems of disease. During 1897 to 1898 a 150 mile region, from Samburu to Makindu, became known as the fly belt; for some 1500 out of 1800 animals used for transport were killed by the tsetse fly, adding further to their problems. Two traction engines were used in some areas where terrain and lack of rain allowed but most equipment and personnel were hauled by train. These early steam engines were fired up by log and wattle burning, causing many a train driver to complain that his engine had indigestion from trying to devour the wrong type of wood! Kenya had no mineral deposits of coal, so any would have to be imported.

1898 saw the railhead reach the Tsavo River, for now 121 miles had then been laid. Because of the water, there was now a proliferation of game available for the cooking pot, which certainly helped the morale of the railhead gang, who also eagerly benefited from the first proper bath in a reasonably sized river. The technicalities of bridging the watercourse were not too difficult, just a realisation that the river in the rainy season would become a raging torrent, so sturdy support columns would be required. However a major additional problem emerged. Two lions started to attack the workers. These were not old or lame animals, unable to catch their normal prey but a pair of healthy and intelligent adult lions who stealthfully came at night and carried off their hapless victims. Traps were set and a vigil kept but the cunning creatures still plucked unwary workers from their very beds! Preston cajoled his men by inferring that the quicker the temporary bridge could be built then the quicker the railhead would proceed away from that area. The main heavily columned bridge system was to be built by the support team following behind the railhead.

Now the main construction team, under the control of Lieutenant Colonel J.H. Patterson, pressed on at the rear, reinforcing bridges and widening cuttings to carry the heavy loads of construction and future freight. So it was their task to build the bridge across the Tsavo River capable of withstanding the full fury of the seasonal flash floods. This would have been a difficult venture anyway considering the location, for the span was to be about 300 ft, the biggest since the Macupa Creek. (It certainly looked very imposing out in the African bush.) However the lion problem persisted even though many soldiers of fortune and amateur hunters appeared in droves to try to capture those astute felines. At one time many Indian workers lay down on the railway line to prevent the train returning to Mombasa, even though the train was only slowed down to a walking pace. Over five hundred men managed to scramble aboard, leaving merely about fifty loyal ones to carry on the construction. Work was effectively halted for three weeks until they were persuaded to go back to work with promises of more protection.

One could understand their concern from the words recorded; *"our contract was to build a railway, not to provide food for the lions!"* The Tsavo lion episode went on for some ten months and claimed the lives of twenty-eight Indians plus an unknown number of Africans. Preston eventually caught one of the lions, almost by accident, for the railhead gang were still not immune from the wandering big cats and Patterson, after much patience, shot the other at Tsavo. A film was made many years later, recalling the saga of the "Tsavo Lions"

There were many other instances of problems with lions. In 1900 at Kima some 260 miles from Mombasa a particularly audacious man-eater absolutely terrorised the area. The local inhabitants eventually persuaded the Superintendent of Railway Police, Charles Ryall to intervene. With two other Europeans they took watch in Ryall's private carriage. One man kept on the watch whilst the other two slept. Evidently Ryall must have dosed off for a moment for the brazen cat entered the carriage, broke Ryall's neck with a strike of it's paw then left through the window with the victim in it's jaws. Eventually a couple of months later the "Kima Killer", as that man-eater became known, was caught again almost as if by accident. There were various other attacks and loss of life, nevertheless none portrayed the craftiness of that of the 'Tsavo lions'. Even after the railway was complete, lions continued to cause 'problems', as seen recorded in an official telegram sent by the 'Babu' (semi-literate Indian station master). *"Please inform station-master Makindu serious mix-up. Approach with caution or beware trouble and life dangers. Four lions with consorts aggressively on platform and completely in charge of my official functions"*

Other animals caused chaos too. Near Simba a herd of rhinos scattered the construction gang and attacked the locomotive. Even though the loco 'won', driving wheel connecting rods were bent! In some areas the heavily creosoted sleepers were still destroyed by white ants, and had to be replaced with steel ones, which got so hot that they burnt the hands of those handling them. At one point caterpillars were so much an infestation that they prevented the train from going up hill because the track was too slippery. A herd of zebra got mired down in the mud of an embankment and almost destroyed it and giraffe caused serious problems with the telegraph poles and wires. Of course we must not forget the antics of the native tribes at that time. Even though there were not many actual attacks on the construction personal, some were particularly vicious. There was also wide spread theft of building materials from the camps and from the lines, for the wire made high quality necklaces and the steel excellent weapons!

Mid 1899 saw the railhead reach the region of what is now the city of Nairobi. It was decided that it was a suitable place to act as a major staging post and depot for the assault on the remainder of that gigantic project. Fed by streams from the hills to the north and west, the savannah of the Athi Plains just teamed with animals, the area was a proliferation of wild life and an abundant source of food for the army of construction workers. Ahead lay the Great African Rift Valley with its 2000 ft escarpments to be negotiated.

Because of the pressure by the railway committee on the time taken, the descent into the Rift Valley was done as a two-fold exercise. The incline was to be built as a staged descending viaduct along the escarpment until level ground was reached. That project alone would take quite a time, so an ingenious scheme was integrated as a temporary way of getting into the Rift Valley itself. The use of a cable incline to enable the carriages and trucks to be winched down on specially designed trolleys had to 'be seen to be believed'! However this meant that progress across the relatively level floor of the valley was able to continue with all speed. The easiest section of the whole railway, until the ascent out on the other side!

During a rare chance of relaxation near the Lake Naivasha area, Preston took the opportunity to do a little hunting and to verify the assumed course of the railway. He spied what he thought were a large number of ostrich eggs on the other side of a small river. On investigation, these white shapes were found to be human skulls, evidently the testament to the massacre of a caravan by the Masai some time before. The macabre site was a sure reminder that they were in dangerous country.

The climb out of the Rift Valley was through dense forest and across deep ravines until the western wall of the valley was breached at Mau Summit at 8700 ft. In contrast to the heat of the desert scrub previously encountered, the torrential rain turned to sleet and the soggy ground caused many derailments. The final 100 miles were often on equally wet ground as if trying to cross the spongy terrain was the last obstacle that Africa could summon up to prevent the railway from reaching its goal. It nearly succeeded for only 6 miles from Lake Victoria an outbreak of dysentery and malaria swept through the construction camp and the heavy rains came and turned the whole area into an absolute quagmire. Trains had to unload whilst still on the move for if they had stopped the heavy engine would have just sunk the rails into the soft embankments. One recorded report talks of a train approaching the rail head as *"coming slowly and cautiously along, rocking from side to side, heaving gently up and down like a ship in a choppy sea-way, and squirting liquid mud ten feet on each side of it"*.

On December 21st 1901 at Port Florence, (now Kisumu) after 582 miles and five years four months, the last rail key was driven home by Florence Preston. This remarkable lady had lived with and supported her husband through the whole project of building the railway from Mombasa.

It now seems hard to believe that 32000 workers were drafted in from India over the five years of that colossal project. Whereas many returned home afterwards, thousands stayed and developed into the large Asian population found in East Africa even today. It was sad that over 2500 people lost their lives during the construction of what was called the 'Lunatic Express'. Writer Elspeth Huxley called it:

"the most courageous railway in the world".

The railway did succeed. The viaducts into the Rift Valley were completed and all the bridge and engineering works finished. Other branch lines were also constructed, adding to the use and profitability of the railway. However many stories were told of the journeys undertaken. For example, sometimes owing to weather conditions the red dust made the lines greasy, so if the train failed to ascend a hill, then the driver would have to return to a level part of the track, let the boiler cool down then build up a good head of steam to try again to the ascend the hill. Sometimes several attempts were made and the whole state of affairs could happen several times so causing the journey from the coast to Lake Victoria to take several extra days! Wise travellers made sure that they carried plenty of food and water. Diesel locomotives eventually replaced the old wood puffers in the early sixties.

Winston Churchhill, who also journeyed on the train in 1907, wrote:

"Through everything...
through the forests, through the ravines,
through troops of marauding lions,
through famine, through war,
through five years' excoriating Parliamentary debate,
muddled and marched the railway;
and here at last, in some more or less effective fashion,
it is arrived at its goal.
And what a road it is".

Chapter 12

Mombasa

The darkness was so intense that it seemed to be unreal. The vast abundance of stars, with the Milky Way stretched like incandescent gauze across the heavens, held me spellbound in the grasp of the magnificence of creation. The moon had gone and there was no light pollution whatsoever for we were seemingly in the middle of nowhere. Looking towards the front of the train, the total blackness had taken on a tinge of deep purple, the sign that dawn would soon be breaking. I woke the others anticipating that they would all like to see the sun rise over the Taru desert. That was almost the last leg of the over night train journey from Nairobi to Mombasa. There were no clouds to spread and reflect the red tint of light back to earth, just the scarlet of the sun's emergence to spread its red glow across the desert. I was still amazed at how quick it all happened. For it only seemed seconds since I was looking at pitch black and now I could see the pink hue on the grey of the thorn trees in such profusion that it looked as if a massive infestation had blighted the landscape. How could this be a desert if there was vegetation, I wondered? As I looked across the stark landscape, there just seemed to be no way through that barrier of lethal thorn. Yes, the Taru had been referred to as a vast waterless torrid plain. It was no wonder that the trade caravans had skirted far to the north to avoid that region. My respect and admiration for the people that built the railway through it, was even more enhanced.

The thorn trees gradually thinned out and the scenery became greener, enabling the lovely sight of palm trees blowing in the gentle breeze among cultivated fields to inspire our eyes away from thoughts of harsh deserts and barren terrain. The long train rumbled across the causeway over Macapu Creek, to get to the small island of nearly 5 square miles, nestled in the estuary on the edge of the Indian Ocean, and then it ground to a halt at the station. Our watches read 8.15 am; we had made up a little time for we didn't expect to arrive until 9 am. The sign on the platform stated 'Mombasa 59 ft'. It was difficult to realise that the bungalow, where we had been staying with Frank's folks, was well over a mile higher than our present location of the ancient city of Mombasa.

Tribal 'cities' along the east coast of Africa had been under the Arab influence for hundreds of years. The Swahili peoples, a result of the Arab and African co-existence, were the ones usually associated in the previous centuries with the trade caravans pushing inland to the 'big waters', where there was a proliferation of ivory, hides and slaves to be obtained for the slave traders of the Middle East. European 'influence' firstly with Portuguese, then the British, left their impression alongside the costume and architecture of the Swahili and Arab peoples. Fortunately the slave trade had virtually ceased and with the railway now offering a quicker and safer journey from the coast to inland locations, the trade brought prosperity to the city and port of Mombasa. We alighted from the train into the hustle and bustle of a multi cultural environment. The colour and noise of the mass of different peoples, with many locals swathed in their brightly coloured 'kanga' wrap around clothing, was in stark contrast to all the other places that we had visited on our travels. Even Nairobi had seemed relatively quiet in comparison, for now more than ever, we seemed like country lads on their first trip to a big city. It was all relative of course for we had sometimes travelled for hours and hardly seen a soul during our explorations. This was certainly a new experience.

We easily managed to obtain a taxi, an old big black Mercedes diesel car, seemingly the bench or trade mark of the taxi business in many parts of the world. The Indian driver pushed through the traffic with the air of authority shown by taxi drivers worldwide. This was his town and he knew everything! Even what time the Likoni ferry sailed; for we would now have to cross over the estuary to the mainland on the south side of Mombasa Island. The small ferry was disembarking, just a few vehicles, but many bicycles and pedestrians heading into town for the days activities. We were going south about 14 miles to a quiet beach resort called Twiga Lodge. As we expected, the single track tarmac soon gave over to a dirt road, which made its way between a mixture of cultivated and wild vegetation and through the occasional village, to show that people did live along there. After about ¾ hour, the car turned left down a rougher track as indicated by a sign stating Twiga Lodge. A mile later we had arrived, virtually right on the beach.

Coffee was served in the bar/restaurant by a smart uniformed bar steward who busied himself with the continuous task of keeping the place spic and span. Ashtrays were filled with sand, which kept the cigarette butt problem to a minimum as they were regularly emptied. Behind the bar itself was a very good child's cartoon framed drawing, reminding everyone that *'children are not allowed in the bar'*. The roof of the building was of thatched palm branches and bamboo with the three sides of the bar room open to the outside with a view only normally seen in films. The one end of the area was literally on the beach, whilst the other two looked out on to swaying palm trees providing shade for a selection of thatched chalets that were scattered about the compound. The long white sandy beach seemed deserted and stretched away into the distance southwards. The other direction saw a rocky headland jutting out into the deep blue sea, as if to keep at bay the coral reef stretching all along that part of the coast. This locality was absolutely beautiful having one of those vistas that I would always remember.

Sylvia Hughes and her husband were the managers of Twiga Lodge, our home for the next week or so. Their son Peter knew Frank from school days (not the same Peter Hughes from Nakuru), so we were soon established into our chalet, built from breezeblock with the traditional thatched roof. It comprised a couple of rooms, one room with twin beds, the main living room also with two beds, plus a bathroom and small kitchenette. The whole set up was more than adequate for our needs. Frank and Peter made a big thing of checking the rafters and rooms for snakes, mainly I felt for the benefit of Bunny, Ian and myself. One tended to live 'al-fresco' in that climate, so we also took advantage of the table in the shade of the biggest bayabab tree that had the biggest girth of any tree I had ever seen, for the four of us could not reach all the way around it. Although not particularly tall, the tree was a mass of branches and leaves; consequently it was also the home of countless creatures! Rumour said that it was so old that it was a sapling when Jesus Christ was born.

On one occasion, Bunny was sitting reading in the living room of the chalet when Frank spied a lizard about 2 ft long, upside down on the wall just above Bunny's head. Poor lad nearly had a heart attack, however lizards are our friends, for they help to keep down the flies and mosquitoes. We still slept under Mosquito nets, even though we took tablets against malaria.

To swim in those clear warm waters with the gentle rollers running up to the beach was a delightful experience. There was hardly any one else about on that long expanse of sand, either. Later we also explored and attempted to snorkel the coral pools around the headland, being very cautious, since we had been warned not too get cut by the coral reef, because infection could soon set in. I was fascinated by the way that the big waves in the rougher water, the ocean side of the reef, pounded against the natural barrier of the coral itself and wondered how any life could survive in that maelstrom. During a long walk down the beach next day we were all amazed by the dugout boats with an outrigger to stabilize the canoe, necessary when negotiating the surf. Frank assured us that those boats ventured out way past the reef and that the local fishermen knew the times and places of when to cross over the reef. It was a very dangerous pursuit. I thought it must have taken a lot of work to build one of those dugout boats and interestingly we saw a number of them only a couple of miles from Twiga Lodge.

The speed at which the weather can change was demonstrated to us that very day. We were enjoying a quiet beer in the bar area when the barman shouted and he quickly began to drop the rolled up coconut matting screens over the open sides of the bar room. We excitedly asked him what was the matter and he just pointed to the open sea. Racing across the ocean were dark menacing clouds with the sign of heavy rain falling, from the grey lines beneath those clouds. By the time he had nearly finished dropping those side screens, the tropical storm was lashing the whole area with high noisy winds and water falling as if from a fire hose. 15 minutes later it disappeared as quick as it had arrived, and we ventured out into the soggy flooded compound. Shortly the sun came back out and within half an hour the ground was dry again!

We decided to hire a car to enable us to explore a bit further afield. So Peter took us into Mombasa in the back of the hotel van and we tried at the main Ford garage to see what their prices were like. They said they did not have any cars available which we did not really believe but I thought 'would I hire a car to four English lads, particularly when there was only a limited amount of good tarmac roads available for travelling on?' We finished up at a back street garage advertising 'Cars for Hire' and ventured into an untidy office occupied by a couple of Indian gents. With our pockets lightened by handing over some Kenyan shillings, the car was brought from round the back and left for us with its engine running. The pale blue Opel Kadet car definitely looked very second hand but we thought at least it was transport. We left the town and headed down to the Likoni Ferry, to make the now familiar short crossing over to the mainland.

The car would not start! The battery was flat! With the expertise of a gang master, Frank soon commandeered some African lads to help us push the jalopy off the ferry and up the ramp to the level ground on top. Then everybody push started the car, which fired into life under threats of being dumped into the sea. We ran inland towards Kwale and explored the Shimba Hills south of the little town, mainly looking for Sable Antelope, which we had been told were often in that area. These antelope were reputed to be the original unicorn, although carried two horns instead of one. Ian thought he spied some up on a ridge over to our left, so with quick instructions to me being the driver at that time to take the track on our left, I literally did so, but did not really appreciate the depth of the gully between the two roads. The car bounced through and when I straightened up after correcting the slide, I realized that the steering wheel now centred in a completely different position. Something must have bent a bit!

We had previously soon discovered that the thing was completely clapped out anyway, so I was not too perturbed by a bent track rod arm. The battery was flat, suspension bushes were worn and dampers very soggy. The brakes were very poor as well, so we were grateful that Frank, when he drove down to the Likoni Ferry was forced to travel slowly behind an old van, otherwise we may have finished up in the water. However we still decided to venture on! A couple of times we had to play with the carburettor or ignition system to keep the old Opel running but it was all part of our African experience.

Now in rural Shropshire I was used to finding animal droppings on the road, usually from cattle or horses, but the size of a pile from a large elephant surprised us all. The track twisted through some trees and then suddenly I hit that large mound of excrement, which flew up and over the bonnet and even dirtied the windscreen. Frank reckoned he hadn't seen a pile that big before but I was more worried about the size and whereabouts of its owner! Where he had got to we fortunately never found out. From a good viewpoint we were able to look across the undulating landscape southwards into Tanganyika (now Tanzania) and again I was just mesmerised by the vast scale of the whole scene. No fences to separate the two countries just a line on a map, which the animals and even many humans took no notice of at all.

We were all invited to visit Frank's old school housemaster and his family who lived near to Jardini about 10 miles south of Twiga Lodge. We swam and surfed the excellent waves rolling on to an exquisite beach. This was probably the best beach that I have ever seen. The white glistening sands, palms trees and sand dunes with the coral reef protecting the inner waters made that coast a very special location. Ian, Frank and I were delighted to have a sail in a little sailing dingy. It was certainly exciting negotiating the surf and I thought of those wooden dugouts that we had seen on our beach. However I was pleased that we did not venture out over the coral, as the ocean was quite rough over on the other side of the reef. We had an excellent lunch and relaxed with stimulating conversation on our hottest day at the coast so far. Yes I was certainly getting to like Mombasa!

Chapter 13

Lorraine

It was a couple of days after our arrival at Mombasa that Peter told us about a do at the water-sports club in town the next evening. I am not sure why, but it ended up with just myself accompanying Peter to the dance. As we bounced back along the typical dirt road to Mombasa, Peter filled me in with some of the colonial customs and niceties as to what happens at these parties. In many ways, the more formal attitudes and manners were in contrast to the so-called permissive society back home in England. But in reality we hadn't seen much of that anyway!

The party was held above the sailing clubhouse, in a spacious room with a balcony stretching along the two sides of the building with excellent views of the estuary and sea; particularly useful for watching boat races. There was a bar at one end of the room and a small stage housing a good, although amateur band, comprising of a piano, guitar, saxophone and drums; as well as a violinist come vocalist who appeared from time to time. An odd assortment, but it quite suited the occasion. The room was well but tastefully lit, so that an observer could see the whole room. Although the do had not been going long, the party atmosphere was starting to warm up. The ambient temperature was very warm anyway, so everyone welcomed the gentle breeze coming through the many open French windows on to the balcony.

I was introduced to quite a few people, of all ages, many of whom had heard about the four mad chaps who had driven over from England! Only half the story again, but it did seem that I was a bit of a celebrity and I didn't like that bit. However, I persisted in polite conversation with different ones without disillusioning them too much!

It was quite common at a dance for girls to dance together, at the start anyway. Now I could not help but notice a certain young lady dancing with some friends. She was very striking. Tallish, about 5ft 7inches and slim, she wore a red flared skirt with gold thread style embroidery on it. I sensed a slightly rebellious spirit, as her skirt was shorter than most of the other more conservative dresses about. It did however show off the best pair of legs that I had seen for a long time and made all the more sensual by her dancing barefoot. Her white blouse also with red and gold embroidery on it, was that as worn by a Spanish flamenco dancer, and was worn off the shoulder showing the lovely golden tan only obtained by a combination of Mediterranean olive oil diet and controlled exposure to the sun. I began to wonder if she had an all over tan!

Her face was pretty with high cheekbones giving her the look of a classic beauty. She had just the correct amount of make up: red lipstick to match her skirt and eye shadow to emphasise those lovely eyes, which seemed to have a sparkle of mischief in them. But it was her hair, which would hold anybody's attention. Shoulder length and the colour of bronze, it was fastened back off her face and allowed to drop down in ringlets, but still keeping the hair off her neck, essential in a hot climate. The style reminded me of that often shown on a Greek goddess, and with the sun having partly bleached some of her hair, she enjoyed the effect of blond highlights, which many a modern woman would pay a fortune for.

As she danced, she moved with the grace and suppleness of a big cat stalking its prey; she certainly had the elegant beauty and body of a young Greek goddess. I was certainly intrigued by the whole scenario and wondered why she wore a pair of very large hoop earrings? Perhaps it was purely for effect as they combined with the flared skirt and off shoulder top to give her the appearance of a very attractive gypsy girl. Peter interrupted my observations and offered to introduce me, had I really been that obvious in looking at the lovely young lady? I guess so.

I was quite embarrassed by his offer, for I was a shy Shropshire lad and felt a little out of my depth. But being quite a strong swimmer I felt I had to do the best I could, as when the music stopped, Peter brought the girl over to me. Her name was Lorraine and she had also been intrigued by my interest in her! After all, I was a celebrity! And it was not often that a stranger appeared at the dance.

Lorraine had a soft lilting type of voice, not the Rhodesian or South African drawl, but an almost too perfect Queens English accent. However it was her smile, which captivated me. She asked me what things were like back home in England, for it had been a few years since she had last visited, and we soon found ourselves chatting and getting along fine, much to my relief!

When the music started again, I asked her "if I might have the pleasure of the next dance" and she replied "Thank you kind sir". (Yes in those days they still played the waltz and quickstep along with some Latin American and rock and roll, so we had the best of both worlds). As I took her hand in mine and placed the other hand around her waist, she automatically placed her left hand on my upper arm and thus we attempted to dance the quick step and in fact, did quite a good job, but I was very conscious of not treading on to a bare foot! Now that she was much closer, I could really sense her perfume. I liked it, but had no idea what it was, and smiled to myself as she danced with the correct 'finishing school' distance between the partners. After a waltz the band changed tune to the Valetta and other progressive dances, aimed mainly at the older generation present, so not wishing to lose my new friend so soon, I offered to buy her a drink, which she eagerly accepted. We walked out on to the balcony, and I felt honoured that she had not released my hand as we stood silently looking at the boats bobbing about in the old harbour under the light of an African moon.

When I returned with the drinks, Lorraine was sitting down on a wicker two-seater settee with a good view of the sea. I was still mesmerised by those legs, which just seemed to go on for ever and now also noted an expanse of thigh exposed by her crossing those legs. She certainly was gorgeous and my thoughts turned to the blouse just hanging off her shoulders as if by magic. We enjoyed our drinks, a sweet martini for her and the local lager for me, only a half though, and chatted away as if we had known each other for quite some time. We jived away to 'Jailhouse Rock' and did the 'Twist'; then we returned to our seat overlooking the sea and chatted away, oblivious to the time.

We were very surprised when suddenly the last waltz started playing and the lights dimmed. As we danced, she moved ever closer and I was able to put both hands around her waist as she moved her arms up on to my shoulders. Our eyes met and we smiled. Now in a hot climate men do not usually wear a jacket and in this case I was no exception, so I was delighted but surprised to feel her body against mine. Her breasts were pert and firm and I could also feel her thighs against mine, and all this aroused feelings in me that were usually very suppressed. I told myself I must behave though and just enjoy the moment while I could. My mind was in a whirl, as suddenly the party was over and taxis and transport had arrived to take people home. We hurriedly arranged to meet the next day, and after a slightly lingering kiss, which tasted sweeter than honey, I watched her get into a car and be driven away. What a night, I had never expected to meet such a beautiful girl, but whether we would meet again or not, I certainly had some happy memories.

On the next day, I thought I had been stood up; for I was on my second cup of coffee and still alone. Lorraine and I had arranged to meet at a pavement café, which was popular with many of the younger Europeans living in Mombasa. I must be at the correct place. "This was Treasury Square?" I enquired again with the waiter. One could not mistake the gigantic crossed elephant tusks, completely over the road, dominating the surroundings, not just one but two pairs had been constructed for the state visit in 1952 of HRH Princess Elizabeth. My watch said nearly midday, when we had arranged to meet at eleven. Well I could have a day on my own sightseeing, I thought, for the whole place seemed quite bustling with activity. The lads did not want me to borrow the hire car, as they were going sailing again near to Tiwi beach down the road. I could have gone too, but the charms of a certain young lady took preference. I thought, perhaps I could get a lift back with Peter's mum, as she had brought me in on her way to the market etc. Nevertheless I did not know where she would be, and anyway, it was too late to go sailing now.

Suddenly, an old large black Peugeot car pulled up in a rush outside the café. Out jumped Lorraine saying that she would explain later but they had to go to the airport. Her eyes were moist and a little red. There had been tears. She introduced me to her mother, who forced a smile with a look that said, "So you are the cause of the trouble are you?" I climbed into the back of the car next to Lorraine and said hello to her two younger brothers and sister, as the car sped away from the café through town and over the Macupa Causeway, connecting the island at the west to the mainland. We reached the airport safely where her sixteen-year-old brother was departing to fly back to Britain for school at Wrexham in North Wales.

He would actually be staying for a few days with Lorraine's grandmother at Ludlow in Shropshire. I hung back trying to be as inconspicuous as possible and not interfere with the family parting. We watched the small plane take off on its way to Nairobi and walked back to the car; we had only just made the flight. At the car, Lorraine's mum offered her hand and introduced herself. "I'm Angela Smith" she said with a slightly warmer smile, "Oh, if only my daughter had explained that she had met someone last night, instead of trying to get out of seeing her brother off to school, then we would not have had such a rush, would we?"

I thought I was ushered into the front seat so Angela could quiz me, "Would you like to come back for some lunch?" she continued, "I am sure Lorraine would like that", she added. I thought I detected a touch of sarcasm? Perhaps not. Now Angela was, I would have guessed, in her late thirties, and I could see from where Lorraine had got her good looks. But she had now exchanged the prettiness of youth for the beauty of a mature woman. Angela was nearly as tall as her daughter and quite slim, and although was obviously very busy with four children to look after, she was still dressed in an attractive manner. Their house was in a nice residential part of the small city, although every one referred to it as 'going to town', and had plenty of grounds and space like the majority of houses there. The gardens were well kept and a showpiece of blooms. We sat on the terrace enjoying a cool glass of homemade lemonade, whilst Angela presided over the preparation of a light lunch. The two children eyed their sister's new friend suspiciously.

Lorraine had explained to me that as I was now open knowledge, in that her mum knew about me, I therefore had to ask her father if I could take Lorraine out in the afternoon, so she could take me sightseeing. She was to be my guide. John Smith was expected back at any time. Well I was learning things, at least we had the same name, but was Angela a Shropshire lass? I hoped so, for that was another point in my favour. They seemed to be cautious of the British attitude to life, particularly with the so-called permissive society, more so predominating the city areas. But, I was a country boy!

I had to formally speak to Lorraine's father when he appeared. After a few minutes he seemed to relax, he didn't know that his daughter had found a friend! He was a tall well tanned man with a reasonable middle aged spread, but seemed quite jovial. I suppose he needed to be with four children to bring up in East Africa. Everyone was on their best behaviour as we enjoyed our lunch and I felt more comfortable as the meal progressed. On his way back to work, John Smith offered to run us up to the old fort, a good starting place for a tour of Mombasa.

Lorraine and I found ourselves at the oldest European bastillion in Africa. The Portuguese built Fort Jesus at the end of the sixteenth century as a protection against the marauding Turks and Arabs, as well as pirates; for Mombasa was at the centre of the East African slave trade. During the heat of the afternoon we looked around the museum then wandered around the fortress before my guide led me down to the old town and the harbour. The narrow streets of old houses in the Swahili style of wooden balconies jutting out, were a frenzy of activity and most interesting.

The Dhows on the estuary river seemed to have been there for centuries, it was certainly another world. Lorraine told me that it could be unsafe to be down by the old port after dark, and in fact, any respectable girl would not just hang around any part of Mombasa at night anyway, so she had told her folks that we would be going to the cinema late afternoon, but that she had to be back home by nine. This could work out well for me too, as Silvia had suggested that I catch the hotel mini bus, which would drop me off at Twiga Lodge on the way back to its base. So, provided I was back at the ferry before nine, there would be no problem. After a bite to eat we walked hand in hand to the lovely park in the centre of town and just enjoyed each other's company.

Lorraine was one of those girls who were so easy to talk to, but always would listen attentively between chattering about anything that came into our minds. She was very knowledgeable. We just got on so well that we hardly noticed the time, so we got hold of a taxi and arranged to meet the next day. The taxi took us down to the Likoni Ferry and the boat was waiting to cross, it was 8.45 pm. After a delicious kiss, I sent the taxi to take Lorraine home, she would not be late; I did not want a reputation of trouble!

Where was the minibus I wondered? No sign of any bus, in fact apart, from a few locals on bicycles, the only vehicle was an old small lorry with three Indian men sitting in the front. The ticket man said that he had not seen the bus either, but that it did not always run every day. I approached the driver of the lorry, as the ferry moved away from the jetty, to ask if I could have a lift. They would take me so far to the point where the road split to Kwale. I would have to walk then. At least it was about half way to the lodge. I climbed on to the back of the truck and sat in the spare wheel on a folded tarpaulin. I did not want the Indians to forget me.

The old lorry bumped its way down the road southward for about thirty minutes and then stopped. This was my get-off point. I thanked them and watched them drive off into the darkness. I was very grateful for the moonlight; at least I could see a little. When there is no moon it is so completely dark. I starting walking at a steady pace; I did not want to exhaust myself too much too soon, for I estimated that I had about ten miles to walk home. There was just no one about, no houses, just the scrub vegetation and the dirt road. The things that a man will do for a pretty gypsy girl!

After about an hour, I heard a motorcycle engine in the distance behind me, a small two-stroke engine, so when I saw the dim light approaching, I tried to thumb a lift. The Vespa rider did not want to know. The way that he was wobbling about, perhaps it was just as well that he did not stop. I carried on walking and eventually saw what looked like a village ahead. The dim lights from the inside of some huts encouraged me, but the only welcome I got was from the barking of a dog alerting its owner to a stranger about. As I was leaving the hamlet behind, there was a rustle in the bushes to the side of the track. My heart missed several beats, for in my naivety I forgot that even though I was not in a game park, this was Africa and wild animals do not know the boundaries. Imagine my relief when the creature that emerged from the bushes was a young domestic calf. But where was its mother? I had seen these cattle and they had long pointed horns; so I hurried on, leaving the calf looking for its mum. A couple of hundred yards down the road I could hear the cow, she had found her calf. I was now more nervous than before and began to hope that I had not missed the left turning, off this track that I needed for Twiga Lodge.

I had no map with me and was trying to memorise the landscape and distances travelled. I was not exactly sure how far I had walked after the lift on the lorry, but it was now gone 11 pm, so I thought I should have at least 4 miles to the turnoff. I was trying to remember if there was a sign, and convinced myself that there was. Having now resigned to walking all the way, I was just determined to push on. I was grateful and very fortunate to still have the moonlight. Then, I heard a vehicle; the unmistakable sound of the air-cooled Volkswagen engine was like music to my ears. I just hoped that they would stop. Yes the Combi-camper van was slowing down, two middle aged German men asked where I was going and I was so pleased to accept their offer of a lift. They said that they were staying at the Jardini Hotel, about 10 miles further along the road, and so I said that if they would drop me off at the track going down to Twiga Lodge, then I would be grateful, for the track was only a mile down to the sea.

"No way" they said, "You should not be walking alone at night down here, and you need to be cautious even in daytime." I wondered why! They explained that a rogue buffalo was causing problems and that the authorities, a policeman and a game warden from Tsavo game reserve were trying to find it. Always finding that the buffalo had left the scene of the carnage before they had arrived. And anyway, there were always lots of other creatures to catch out unwary travellers. They insisted on taking me right down to the lodge itself. I was pleased for their insistence, for now more than ever, I knew what a stupid thing it was to just walk home as if I had been in Shropshire.

On leaving me at the lodge they asked if I was going to the barbecue and dance at the Jardini Hotel, the day after tomorrow. That would be our last night in Mombasa, so I said to them that I would tell my friends about it. It sounded a good idea, particularly if a certain gypsy girl could go! As I turned to walk to the chalet, I was met with an awe-inspiring sight. A tall jet black native wearing a kaki British army battle dress top, a kikois, a (wrap-around style skirt), with a bow and quiver of arrows over his shoulder and carrying a panga in his hand, (a large long bladed chopper used for hacking through brush or used as a weapon if necessary) and a fez on the top of his head to complete his uniform, was on duty as the night watchman! Fortunately he spoke English and had seen me about before. I am sure that I would have remembered him though!

I arrived back at Lorraine's house about 10.30 am the next morning as arranged. I asked Frank to wait for a moment so I could check if everything was still ok. The lads were going to explore the north coast for a change and had given me a lift to Mombasa. I think they were curious about my new friend, and wanted to see if she was really as gorgeous as I had told them. Peter had been stirring it a bit as well, so I was the subject of a lot of leg pulling, especially over having to walk back home to the lodge. Angela opened the door and looked at me, and then at the three musketeers in the old Opel Kadet hire car. I could tell from her expression what she thought! But she actually invited me in, so a thumbs up to the lads and off they went, disappointed at not having seen the gypsy girl yet.

I sat on the terrace drinking yet another cup of coffee, chatting to Angela whilst waiting for her daughter. Lorraine appeared, then her mother said, "I wondered why you were after the sowing machine." but with a look that told us both that – the skirt is a bit too short. She had that amazing capacity of stating things with just a look, and she was always right too. Angela moved across to her daughter and put her arm around her shoulders.

"I was young and foolish once, but you will just have to learn won't you? Just make sure that you behave." And then she mouthed at me "And you too." I couldn't help but smile, trying to do as she did, by conveying the thought "but I always behave", but I don't think she believed me!

"And what are you two going to get up to today?" the question took us both by surprise.

"Sightseeing" we said meekly.

"Well I think that it would be a good idea for John to come back for tea, as you won't want to see the same film again, will you?" Angela obviously knew all the tricks, and no one could pull the wool over her eyes. Yes I thought, I bet she was even more mischievous than her daughter.

I plucked up courage and told them about the barbecue at the Jardini Hotel and suggested that if Lorraine wished to bring a friend or two, then that would be great. Angela surprisingly agreed, safety in numbers perhaps. So I cheekily suggested that if they would like to come over to Twiga lodge, then they could have the whole day there and then go on to the barbecue. In for a penny in for a pound! I had not even had chance to ask Lorraine, perhaps she would not want to go, but the look on her face said otherwise.

"You had better do some quick arranging my dear," said Angela, I was getting to like her as well.

The day was spent with more sightseeing, (well the sight of Lorraine in a sleeveless summer dress was certainly a sight worth seeing). It was another beautiful day, but I do not remember much of the different things that we had explored, just that my guide's company was absolutely exquisite. We returned for tea as instructed. I did not want to spoil the chance of another day with my lovely new girlfriend. We were both getting quite fond of each other. The evening passed by all too quickly, but I did notice that Lorraine was a lot more reserved in front of her parents; but I should have expected that. She did however keep trying to make me laugh by inappropriate use of her foot under the table.

Eventually, I had to leave in order to catch the ferry. I welcomed the chance of a taxi ride back to the lodge, even though it cost money, as I did not relish the repeat walk back home! A taxi was called and I said thank you to Angela and John Smith for their hospitality. They sportingly allowed us a few moments to say goodnight in the porch whilst awaiting the taxi. Oh those kisses, they were certainly sweeter than the finest nectar. We were both looking forward to the day at Twiga Lodge tomorrow.

I had told Frank, Ian and Bunny about the barbecue at the Jardini Hotel just a few miles down the road. Most of the holiday places were located along the coast, north of Mombasa at Malindi, with just the occasional establishment on the south side. This made it usually very quiet. We actually counted nine people on the long, long beach the other day! As it was to be our last night at Mombasa, we all decided to go, Frank, Bunny, Ian, Peter and I. I told them that I had arranged for Lorraine and a friend to come over to Twiga Lodge to spend the day there before going on to the barbecue that evening. When she arrived with three girlfriends, it certainly put a smile on the lad's faces, and it was not long before we were all in the sea enjoying a swim and then an attempt to play water polo with a soft beach ball.

Many people might have thought that girls versus boys was unfair, and I did wonder at first; for I had played a bit whilst at school and water polo can get a bit rough. Bunny, not being a particularly good swimmer, volunteered himself to referee from the shallows and no one seemed perturbed by there being no goal posts either, so these had to be imaginary, and I laughed to myself about the impending arguments.

What I did *not* know was that three of the girls were strong swimmers and two had played water polo before. I knew Lorraine could swim ok, but not how good. But the factor, I just failed to recognise at the start, was the effect of four lovely young women in bikinis splashing about in the water, would have on the concentration of the lads to the actual game of water polo! We just never stood a chance!

Lorraine had no qualms about grabbing me around the neck, or else where, to stop me from reaching the ball, and my gypsy girl was a very quick swimmer indeed and as slippery as an eel too, difficult to catch. It was not long before the lads were losing, so desperate measures were needed. The girls were fouling constantly, (for you are not supposed to grab hold of your opponent!) so I suggested to our team that we should not play so gentlemanly!

When a swimmer reaches the ball, in order to throw it back from their side, they will turn with arm outstretched and hand under the ball to use the full leverage of the arm to get maximum distance of throw, but in that position they are most vulnerable to attack. I noticed that Lorraine and her friend Sue, short for Suzanne, were doing that. They had played before. It was not long before the chance came for me to act not quite so sportingly! Lorraine was just turning with arm outstretched to throw the ball when I arrived quickly, but instead of stopping and trying to block the throw, I just turned on to my side and sliced through between her and the ball. The body weight is enough to 'accidentally' push the other person under the water, but it is then easy to allow yourself to sink and take your opponent down deeper. Very naughty really, for I was expecting it and she wasn't. I didn't feel too guilty though, as I had lost count of how many times Lorraine had already ducked me under the water. However, my conscience prevailed and I quickly grabbed her round the waist with one arm and swam with her back to the surface, I hadn't realised how deep the water was at that spot. My coughing and spluttering little friend was not the happiest of creatures for a few moments, but then she playfully hit me and muttered something about getting her own back. But that was all that I had done!

We all needed a short rest, as the sport is quite tiring and it was starting to get a bit physical, so a suggestion was made about changing the match to beach volleyball. The girls, having been in conference, protested and offered another 10 minutes, to give the boys chance to catch up! So we all continued with renewed vigour. However, I did not trust these scheming felines, and swam very cautiously, trying to always see what Lorraine was doing, but being shortsighted and not being able to wear my glasses in the water, I was at a distinct disadvantage. I had not even got the ball, when the attack was launched with the skill and swiftness of three young lionesses running, or swimming, down their prey. I just never stood a chance, I could have managed one, probably coped with two, but the three, nubile and feisty girls overwhelmed me!

I was pushed down under the water and usually that is it, but they kept pushing me further down, so I grabbed one of the girls and pulled her down with me, for if you go deep you can usually swim out of trouble. Someone was trying to free the girl from my grasp and only succeeded when the instigator of this frenzy took my head in her hands and kissed me on my lips to claim victory! We all surfaced breathless and exhausted, with no casualties other than my pride. They had certainly got their own back! As we swam and then walked to the shore, the others were still laughing at the scenario. I complained to them about not having any help, but Frank commented that they couldn't help for laughing and anyway they said that I seemed to be enjoying the scrap!

Most seemed to have had enough of swimming, so we left Allana and Tania to entertain, or be entertained by the lads, as all seemed to be getting on fine. As Lorraine and Sue had brought their fins and masks and Peter had lent me some, the four of us wandered to the left end of the beach by where the coastline turned to the rocky outcrops; which is always a good spot for snorkelling. With the added bonus of the reef being quite close to the rocks at that point, we hoped to find plenty to see. *(We had been warned to not touch anything and to be cautious on the reef anyway, as a cut from the live coral will quickly go septic. However, the big advantage of the reef is that it keeps big fish such as sharks and barracuda away from the beach area, so swimming is relatively safe. It was not until many years later, when I was persuaded to invest in a mask with my own prescription lenses fitted, that I was to fully appreciate that wonderful world under the sea. We have all been spoilt, by watching wildlife and travel, to exotic places, on film and television, but to actually see and experience it first hand is something that I strongly recommend to anyone who has the chance to go.)* So it was a fitting finale to compliment the many wonders of mainland Kenya that I had seen, to again look at the underwater world of the East African Coral Reef.

I was standing in about 4 ft of water trying to readjust my mask when Lorraine, touching my arm, motioned me not to move. On looking down I saw a long green and creamy/white sea snake gliding between my legs and was quite petrified. I don't like snakes at the best of times, but knew that sea snakes are more poisonous than even normal ones. I was greatly relieved when the snake continued on its way and ignored the trespasser in its territory! We all continued to snorkel our way along and round the rocky outcrop into a tiny bay, which was full of small fish of every conceivable shape and colour. Avoiding the spiky sea urchins, which when dead reveal their beautiful round shells often seen in gift shops, we climbed out on to the rocks and watched the tide still receding and now exposing the great coral reef. I was amazed at how calm the sea was on our side of the reef but how rough it seemed out to sea. Evidently when there is a tide surge, the sight of the sea breaking over the reef is most spectacular. It was one of those moments that I will never forget. Sitting on the rocks with a beautiful girl leaning back against me and watching the great reef slowly seeming to rise out of the sea in a kaleidoscope of colour.

The others called us, as evidently lunch was nearly ready, so we hastened back to the lodge, and not before too long, as I could really feel where the sun had caught my skin. Peter's mum, Sylvia, had generously arranged for lunch for us all, alfresco style, around the good-sized table under the old mgumu tree. A quick shower under the popular beach type system, comprising a five-gallon drum up a tree filled with fresh water, and to operate it, one pulled a cord to let the water fall through a valve and an old watering can rose. Well it worked and the sun had even warmed the water. One had to be quick though, before the water ran out, so I did not mind sharing my shower with Lorraine! At least it washed the salt off our skin and out of our swimwear.

Luncheon was quite a simple affair, not because of a lack of hospitality by Sylvia, but because we were all going to the barbecue later at the hotel down the road. Fresh bread, some cooked meats and some cheese, were served by the waiter from the Twiga Lodge restaurant and drinks were brought by the barman, both neatly attired in their uniforms. I have had a philosophy that memorable meals can be like milestones on our journey through life, and this luncheon was no exception; for it is the company, which is the important factor. As I looked around the table at the ten people all enjoying the occasion, everyone seemed at ease, and the conversation was lively and interesting as we talked about our stay in Africa and our thoughts of the future. Often in a gathering, one or two people will tend to dominate the proceedings and like to be the centre of attention, (which is probably why I enjoy smaller groups) but that was certainly not the case here. Everyone seemed to be able to chat away in turn or in their own little conversations with their neighbour. As I looked around the table at the different characters, I wondered what would become of each one in the future and wished them all well. All but the snorkellers had changed, but no one had wanted to wait for lunch any longer, so we looked a mixed bunch anyway. A middle-aged lady, five young men in their twenties and four pretty girls all enjoying each other's company. That is what memorable meals are about.

When the conversation again got around to the coffee plantations, that were ever more becoming available for sale, Sylvia suggested that we should buy one between us, as we would soon master the expertise needed. Lorraine, who was snuggled up close, squeezed my hand in encouragement and thought it was a great idea. We all certainly had a lot to think about, as this subject had been raised several times during our stay and so we talked about the proposed venture well into the afternoon. I wonder what would have happened if we had given up our families in England and become farmers in Kenya?

The girls decided that it was time for them to get ready for the evening. How long did they want? Being gentlemen we said that they could use our chalet to change in, but a time limit of an hour was mentioned, one bathroom and four girls, that was optimism! We continued to talk about the farm and the changing political scene in East Africa and a couple of us were very tempted, but it was not to be. We had to chase the girls up as the rest of us needed to get ready for the evening, but Frank and Ian used the house facilities, which certainly helped the time factor. The girls certainly looked very nice and did us proud. It is amazing how a pretty skirt can show off a pair of legs to perfection, even though we had been looking at the girls in bikinis all day. Men will never understand the effects of women! We lads now had to make a big effort as well. But I had only got two pairs of shorts and that is what most men would wear to an outside do.

The ox roast was nearly done when we arrived in two cars: ten of us, as Sylvia decided to join us as well. The dance floor was a smoothed out area of the beach, marked out by logs in a square, which also doubled as extra seating. Coloured lights were strung around some trees and the local band provided the music. The party was just starting to warm up and we were soon tucking into delicious meat, roast potatoes and local salad with all the trimmings. I felt that a very pleasant night was in store to round off a beautiful last day at Mombasa. We ate, danced, enjoyed a glass of wine and danced some more before going for a walk barefoot on the beach and down to the sea, illuminated by a full African moon. It seemed twice as big down by the Equator, an optical illusion I know, but twice as bright as well. The sparkle of the moonlight on the waves breaking on to the great coral reef was very romantic, particularly with the company of my beautiful gypsy girl. She was wearing the same outfit that she wore when we first met, and if I had been captivated then, now I was just mesmerized.

Strolling with our arms around each other and the water lapping over our feet we were both oblivious as to how far we had walked. I just felt that Lorraine wanted to kiss as much as I did, so stopping, I held her close: her lips eagerly sought mine and I am sure that we created a world record in how long it lasted! It seemed to go on forever, that lovely kiss of pure affection. We strolled back up the beach and lay back on a sand dune to watch the tide coming in, for the waves were now getting bigger and noisier out on the reef.

This was perfection. This was paradise. The giant rollers racing in from the Indian Ocean were crashing against, and being sent skywards by the great coral reef. The moonlight picked out the surf and it all sparkled in a 'son ét lumier' that only nature can provide. I wondered if there would be a tide surge tonight. She snuggled very close and I could feel the curves of her body against mine. We clung to each other, never wanting that moment to end; we were just overawed by the power of nature. The noise of those rollers out on the reef was increasing as each wave thrust itself against the coral in an effort to break through to the calmer waters of the bay. Each wave caused the tide to rise higher and higher until in a crescendo of noise and activity, the tide surge broke over the reef and raced to the shore in a frenzy of one wave after another, finally expiring on the beach.

The next day saw all of us very subdued. We were to catch the train back to Nairobi that evening and then it would not be long before our long journey back to England. We had seen so much and done so much that the whole adventure now seemed like we had just read about it in a book. But it had actually happened. Four ordinary young men had done the journey and adventure of a lifetime. All we had to do now was to travel back home! We just mooched about a bit as we were all late getting up. We had a swim, packed and said our farewell to Peter and his mum Sylvia, and thanked them for all they had done. For a last time we went back to the Likoni ferry and into Mombasa; deposited our cases at the railway station then returned the hire car, thankfully in one piece. Then we got ready for the long train journey through the night.

I had said my goodbyes to Lorraine at the hotel. It was very late when we returned from our walk and many had already gone home from the barbecue. Sue and the girls were starting to worry where we had got to, but Frank assured them that I was quite capable of looking after Lorraine! As the girls were all staying with Sue, they would only, hopefully, have to explain their lateness to one set of parents.

We were sitting in the carriage with plenty of time before the departure when, who should appear at the door but Lorraine. The lads all smiled and said their goodbyes, so I ushered her to the end of the carriage where we could be afforded a little privacy. We hugged and kissed and looked into each other's eyes, hers were watering and I felt mine doing so too. I gently brushed away a tear with my lips and did not mind the slightly salty taste, and then another tear from the other cheek. I was so pleased to see her, but somehow knew that this would be the very last time that we would see each other. I thought that it was a Lakeland poet who said, 'That parting is such sweet sorrow'. I now knew what he meant. The patient guard finally helped Lorraine down off the train, which immediately started on its way. I leaned out of the window and we waved at each other, but I was surprised to see Angela walk forward and put her arm around the shoulders of her daughter and they were both still waving as the train moved out of sight. What a loving, understanding and compassionate mother Angela certainly was.

Chapter 14

Trains, Planes and Automobiles.

I hardly noticed as the train crossed the Macupa causeway and trundled on its way up towards the Taru desert. We were all very quiet, all deep in our special memories of Mombasa. Frank passed me another cigarette and commented, "You are very fond of that girl, aren't you?" 'Yes' I thought and 'I don't think I will ever forget her'. It was not long before the light faded and it was just total darkness outside, nothing to interrupt my recollections, not just of Mombasa and Lorraine, but of the whole African experience. Well in fact the whole trip, for the long journey too, had been an adventure and I was saddened to think that it would not be long before we would start on that extensive drive back through Europe to Stafford.

Again we enjoyed an excellent dinner on the train and even with; perhaps an extra bottle or two of the local Tusker ales, I found it was still difficult to sleep. We had seen so much and done so much that the whole exploit seemed almost unreal, as if we had just read about it all in a book or had been told it all by a good storyteller. I thought about that mammoth trek from Stafford to Athens, and all those different encounters. The journey through France and Germany, then the primitive night halt we had in the Austrian Alps. I thought of the austereness of Yugoslavia and the bureaucracy of Greece. We had certainly experienced life even before we arrived in Nairobi.

Then Africa. To me Kenya was a country of contrasts. I loved the game parks where we had been able to see many animals in their natural habitat. The White Highlands gave us an insight into the traditional colonial life as practised by the farming and estates communities. The experience of spending the night at Tree Tops was another unforgettable memory; for how could anyone not remember the sounds of the bush at night? The Great African Rift Valley emphasized the power of nature and just how fragile the earth can be. The contrast of beautiful lakes full of life, to the extreme hostile soda waters of another lake a few miles away, could only be found in Africa. The volcano and drama of Hells Gate were permanently etched on my mind. The interesting train journey to the coast and the exquisite beaches and environs of Mombasa, all added to make our visit to Kenya a truly great experience. Thoughts of Mombasa obviously stirred up memories of Lorraine, so I guess I must have dropped off to sleep dreaming of the charms of my delectable guide.

Back at the Rothera's bungalow the next day, our thoughts turned to planning for our trip back home and to do the things that we had yet to do. Like shopping for presents. The weeks had just flown by and we were shortly to be flying back to Athens. We confirmed our bookings for the flight and all was ok; nice surprise! We decided to buy a gift for David and Edna Rothera as a token of our gratitude for their excellent hospitality and for all the help that they had given to us to make our trip of a lifetime so special. We invested in an elephant's foot, which had been made into a container with a polished hardwood top and we had a little plaque suitably inscribed with our names and the date of our visit. *(In the 1960s these types of ornaments were made from dead animals to also raise income towards conservation in the game parks. Even though poaching still happened, animals were not then needlessly killed for mementoes. Today because of international pressure that practice is now rare.)*

The other thing that we had to get was the genuine Kenyan black honey for the doctor who had given to us the necessary inoculations for our tropical venture. Frank's dad had heard of it, although he didn't know where to get any from, he suggested our friend the farmer Jack Stevens. Jack joined us all for a meal and another interesting evening, when we also viewed a couple of the films of slides that we had taken. "Are you sure that he asked for the old Kenyan black honey?" Jack asked. We explained about the doctor serving with the RAF in Kenya and that brought a mischievous smile to the weather beaten face of the old farmer. "Well if that is what he wants, then leave it with me!" We were all still mystified and wondered what we would be carrying back home for the doctor. Next day when he appeared with a pot of the stuff we could understand his query, for the jar contained not only the almost black sticky liquid but honeycomb and dead bees as well! "Leave it all just as it is" said Jack and wished us all a good journey and an interesting future. He was certainly a character.

We said our goodbyes to David and Edna Rothera on our departure, then Frank took us to the airport. He was to follow on in a few days. The Air Alitalia DC8 took off in the darkness at 12.44 am on its non-stop uneventful flight to Athens, where we landed at 6.30 am local time. After clearing the formalities and a taxi ride to the contact flat in Athens, we met up with Dave, who had been so helpful in dealing with the Greek officialdom. He took us over to get the car unsealed from out of the customs approved garage, where we were delighted to have the car handed over to us with no trouble at all. A flat tyre was the only problem! An afternoon swim at the beach that Bunny and Ian had previously discovered, was followed by a meal in an outdoor restaurant in the Plarca area of Athens. Then we settled into the cheap but reasonable hotel that Dave had recommended to us during our brief stay in the city. 10/- (50 pence) each was reasonable at any rate.

At 9.30 am on September 10th 1966 we drove out of Athens under a clear blue sky with the weather still hot, but we were grateful, for it was not the extreme heat we endured on our outward journey. During the afternoon in northern Greece we experienced the first problem with the car. Carburettor flooding, so, while sitting on the side of the road, I made some new gaskets out of brown paper, whilst Bunny, with Ian's supervision, stripped the carbs to find the problem. We generally thought that it was some dirty fuel taken on in Yugoslavia, by the amount of fine sediment in the float chambers. How much had settled in the bottom of the fuel tanks during our stay in Kenya we did not know but we certainly hoped that it was not a lot. We continued northwards and into Yugoslavia without any problems so I thought that the relative stamps in our passports from our outward journey helped to speed up the border crossings.

An evening meal at a motel near to Skopje was only marred by the very slow service of the waiters; therefore we seemed to have lost a lot of the time that we had saved at the border! We survived yet again the concrete autoput, even though thick fog was prevalent in the early morning. Then we again had carburettor problems, this time from fuel starvation. The carbs were again removed and in Bunny's words, "effected a more permanent cure". A lousy breakfast at the motel at Zagreb disappointed us, after the good evening meal we had had a few weeks previously, nevertheless afterwards we just carried on northwards.

Yet again we climbed over the summit of the Loibl Pass and entered Austria in the afternoon, then on to Klagenfurt. At last we were travelling on a good sweeping road descending from the mountains to the valley below, and were now pleased to be making good progress with about half the journey completed. A loud banging noise spoilt the illusion of contentment. A drive shaft coupling was breaking up and a rattle on the suspension was also getting worse. We limped into Klagenfurt and parked up by the railway station. I thought that Ian must have reckoned that if we couldn't fix the car then at least we were next to a train! However whilst Ian went walkabout, I helped Bunny change the 'doughnut', drive shaft coupling, and sort out the rattling suspension. We were soon on our way over the other mountain passes without problems, therefore we decided to stop at Salzburg for an evening meal. A pleasant open-air establishment on the bank of the river served us well, even though we did not sample the local brew. During the meal we decided to travel on again through the night as we, and the car, all seemed fit and raring to go. The German border was crossed about 9 pm and in contrast, now most of the route lay on good motorways.

Driving continuously through the night in two-hour stints meant that good progress was made. No more mechanical problems to slow us, although we were plagued with thick fog at times. On through Luxembourg, for we changed route and headed for the Belgium border, which we crossed at 7 am and on to the port of Oostend. On arrival at the ferry terminal, Ian went to check that our tickets were ok and to find out when the next boat was sailing. He waved us forward, jumped back into the car and said that the officer told us to hurry and follow the directions being waved at us. We were all very surprised to suddenly board the ferry, and before we had got out of the car, the giant deck doors closed and we were on our way out into the North Sea. We just looked at each other and could hardly believe Ian's analysis; "2000 miles in 48hrs. Not bad, eh?" That time also included all stops and breakdowns, for it was just two days ago that we had left Athens.

The 4hr sea crossing to Dover enabled us all to get some sleep before tackling the last leg of our journey home. The customs officials at Dover were interested in our having Kenyan stamps in our passports and also having African souvenirs when we had arrived on the ferry from Belgium! We explained and then arose the question of Ian's camera lens, when he was given a lecture how the dealers give a receipt for a lower value in order to mean paying less tax on entry to UK. "Do they really?" exclaimed Ian but was pleased to get away with £12 duty. After clearing the formalities, we managed to phone our respective families to inform them that we were at last back on British soil. They all seemed very relieved. Two hours of London rush hour traffic was certainly a return to the reality of England and then when we managed to join the M1, we came across the only major traffic accident that we had seen during the whole trip. At the service station for yet another meal, Ian confused the coloured lady serving the food with a cheerful greeting in Swahili "jambo". She hadn't got a clue what he meant. Perhaps she was from Jamaica?

We continued on the very last leg of our mammoth journey and then as the car pulled up back at Sun Cottage near Stafford, the sound of the car on the gravel drive alerted our neighbours and landlords, Geoff and Irene Grypton, who soon came out to welcome us home, with cries of "well we did wonder if we would ever see you all again!"

When Frank arrived back at Sunco, then the four of us went to take the doctor his honey. We were invited in to his home and he looked most surprised. For we had not only remembered to get the honey but we had managed to obtain the genuine article, complete with the honeycomb and dead bees. We said that we were perturbed by the bees but nevertheless told to leave them in the jar. The doctor reckoned that the bees added to the 'flavour' and fermenting although one didn't normally eat them!

A couple of days later, I was delighted to receive a long chatty letter from Lorraine, and in fact we communicated for many, many months. I felt that it was an interesting coincidence that, less than two years later, Frank and I went over to France to compete in our first international car rally, a French alpine event called

'Rallye de Lorraine'- but that's another story!

Chapter 15

The Slide Film Show

It was now time for us to fulfil our obligation to the education personnel of the English Electric Co. We had been given extra leave to enable us to make our special trip to Africa, so now in return we had to give a lecture on our experiences, at the College of Technology at Beaconside, Stafford. That was a daunting task for anybody, never mind for four young men who had never given a lecture before. Between us we had taken hundreds of slides, so from the thoughts of using slides, during the lecture in any case, developed the idea of actually doing a slide show as our presentation.

Now Ian came from a very keen photographic family and had previously visited, with his parents, a Kodak slide show presentation, which used multiple projectors to give a very special effect. As we were all impoverished students, we only owned, between us, one Leitz manual slide projector, so we had a long way to go! We had been kindly lent a Ferograph series 4 stereo tape recorder. This would enable us to record a commentary, because at that time, not one of us felt capable of speaking on a live presentation. Peter Rogers, the photographic specialist in Stafford, were persuaded to lend to Ian their demonstration remote control Leitz Pradavit slide projector, which was identical to the one they had supplied to the college for lecture purposes.

Hence, there evolved the system of using two remote control projectors, showing alternative slides and supported by a pre-recorded sound commentary and perhaps suitable background music too. The problem now was to effect a system so that each projector could be faded in and out when required. *(In 1966 projector bulbs were still carbon filamented and relied upon heat build up to provide the light intensity needed so they could not just be switched on and off. Modern halogen bulbs can be dimmed electronically.)*

A mechanical fader, or shutter mechanism was therefore necessary, and Bunny was delegated to develop the device! His ingenuity came to the fore, and while Ian, Frank and I tried to format some sort of order for the slides and the basis for a script, Bunny beavered away in the workshop on his mechanical masterpiece. A windscreen wiper motor, from off a scrapped Midland Red bus standing at Snows Yard in Stafford, was used to provide the oscillating back and forth motion so that a shutter could be opened or closed in front of either projector as needed. A shutter comprised of two plates, which opened or closed like an iris on a very simple camera. By progress it was discovered that by shaping the inside edges into a curve, then the slide was faded away without any shadow lines moving across the picture. With an identical shutter opening in front of the second projector, then that slide emerged into a full picture to replace the previous one.

The effect was quite remarkable, for now a slide or scene change was effected without shadow lines or a darkened or white screen to spoil the appearance of the show. In practice black slides were used when necessary, so that the pictures at the start and finish of the performance just faded from and back to the blank screen. Rather like a scene change in a film where one scene fades into another. A series of night shots, of the road lit up by the car headlamps, used on the journey to Athens, almost looked like cine film as each slide was constantly faded into the next giving the illusion of movement. The whole scene only lasted a few seconds but was quite dramatic.

This mechanical slide picture dissolver unit then had a relay/electronic logic system added, designed by Bunny of course, so that synchronisation of the slide changing of the relevant automatic projector was possible. Slides had to be sorted into the relevant slide cassette trays, odd numbers in one and even numbers in the other, as of course, the first slide was being shown from projector one with the second slide, already lit up behind the shutter, from projector two. The projector in waiting changed its slide when instructed to do so!

With the slides sorted into order, a commentary was recorded on to the Ferograph tape recorder. It was eventually decided to use Ian's voice for the journey or first half of the show, and Frank's voice for the Kenya exploration. Music from Bert Kamfert's 'Swinging Safari' was deemed to be a good basis for the African section and so a lot of time was spent mixing and stretching music to fit the appropriate scene. The commentary and music were then amalgamated on to the one track of the stereo tape. This was so that the lower track could be used to carry a tone burst, which would indicate to the slide dissolver unit when it was to instigate the next slide. This meant of course that any slide could be kept on screen for the exact time predetermined, essential when the reading of a plaque or a particular good photograph of an animal was being shown. In reality it was perhaps surprising that, with very few exceptions, each slide was shown for only a few seconds.

We were very grateful for the co-operation of the staff at the college and to Peter Rogers Photographic for their help. Bunny was under strict instructions not to modify any of the borrowed equipment, so an element of extra wiring and sundry bits were all added to enable the show to go on. The whole collection was originally designed for just the one performance at the College of Technology. We were all surprised that the lecture theatre was so full of friends and fellow students from English Electric and the college. My parents and some friends from Market Drayton also attended. Apart from the embarrassment of a fan belt breaking on one of the projectors which meant a slight delay whilst a hair dryer to blow cold air was acquired, the show went well with the journey half being about 30 minutes, a 15 minutes break and the Kenya part about 45 minutes. Bunny then gave a short explanation of the technicalities of the way the show had been presented.

Ian did buy the Leitz Pradavit projector from M/s Peter Rogers and I bought his old Leitz manual projector, which is still going strong. The slide show was performed a couple of times at Market Drayton for a Rotary Club Charity event and was also of course shown in Yorkshire, Bunny and Ian's home county. In various forms it was also shown to some schools and other organisations. We never expected such a demand for our 'lecture', but the uniqueness of the production of such a slide show back in 1966 was certainly a credit, particularly to Ian and Bunny.

After such an interesting and adventurous trip, coupled with the time taken to prepare the slide show presentation, it may be thought that everything that followed would be an anticlimax. However, the RAC Rally, Britain's premier international car rally, was looming up fast, and we had volunteered to marshal on it. I wondered at that time whether I would ever have the opportunity to compete.

Perhaps one day!

The End.

174

Post Script
&
Acknowledgements

After our African adventure, other continental trips and an increasing involvement in motor sport, it seemed incongruous that Ian should have been tragically killed in a car accident close to his home near Stafford in October 1968.

Frank moved to South Africa and worked, as an electrical engineer, with Zambian Consolidated Copper Mines associated with Anglo American, and continued to work mainly in Africa even after he settled in Kent. Andrew joined Lucas Racing division and he was the brains behind the electronic ignition systems for the Cosworth V8 'Formula-1' racing engines of the 1970s. I went into the motorcycle trade for a few years and still competed in different motor sport events from time to time.

In April 2006 I was grateful of the opportunity for Frank, Andrew and myself to meet up and spend the night at Frank's home in Kent after a gap of many, many years. Consequently it was with those memories of the three of us from forty years ago that I was able to confirm and correct some of the detail of this story. I had a distinct advantage since I had already been working on the book for a year or so! Nevertheless it was a very nostalgic and memorable occasion with of course the mandatory photograph of the three of us with the elephants foot which we had given to Frank's parents at the end of our stay in Kenya. I was also grateful to Andrew for lending me his little diary, which I didn't know he had kept, from which I was able to validate many of the dates, places and names of people that we had met, along with snippets of other interesting and amusing information. Andrew had also kept the African part of the slide show, from which on seeing it again I was able to add to my compilation of memories from my own slides.

Obviously a lot of interesting research was undertaken to add some background history into our story. As I was so intrigued by the tale of the building of the Kenyan railway, I felt I must share that legend with you. Charles Miller's very readable book 'The Lunatic Express' also gives a dramatic detailed history of East Africa prior to the railway but here I am only able to share a little of the story of that memorable construction. Mrs. Glenys Jones, granddaughter of Ronald and Florence Preston, had lived the latter part of her life in Stafford and had donated many photographs and souvenirs, known as the Preston collection, to the Oxford University Museum.

I would like to extend a special thank you to Amanda Burdett, not only for the inspiration to write this book but also for the considerable help and advice, which has enabled me to actually put pen to paper.

My many thanks also to my sister Janet Abrahams who had the painstaking and arduous task of proof reading. A new red pen is appropriate I think!

And finally a big thank you to my wife Hazel for the support and encouragement she has given, to enable me to complete this literary venture.

Photographs. I also thank the Kenya Tourist board for use of the 'Portrait of a Lion' and 'Longonot' pictures featured in their 'MagicalKenya' web site. Other photos were selected and renovated from our original slides taken 40 years ago!

Maps and Covers were drawn and compiled by the author.

John Abrahams. © 2006.

Printed in the United Kingdom
by Lightning Source UK Ltd.
114999UKS00001B/127-189